THE STATE OF MAN - *what the Bible says*

by

Jude Njoku

Published by

NEW GENERATION PUBLISHERS
Lagos, Nigeria

Printed in the Federal Republic of Nigeria

by

NEW GENERATION PUBLISHERS
13, Akinyele Street, Aguda, Surulere,
Lagos, Nigeria
ISBN 1-60034-193-4
Phone: 234-1-8034094666
E-mail: newgeninworld@yahoo.com

The state of man

TABLE OF CONTENTS

INTRODUCTION

1.   HOW DID DEATH COME ABOUT?

2.   WHERE DO THE DEAD GO?

3.   THE SOUL

4.   SPIRITUALISM

5.   RESURRECTION

6.   FOR THE LIVING

ALL SCRIPTURAL QUOTATIONS

ARE TAKEN FROM

THE AUTHORISED KING JAMES VERSION

OF THE HOLY BIBLE

ACKNOWLEDGEMENT

I thank God immensely for the Excellency
of His wisdom

The state of man

DEDICATION

Dedicated to all lovers of the truth of the Gospel.

The state of man

Revelation 22:18, 19 "For I testify unto every man that heareth the words of the prophecy of this book. If any man shall add unto these things, God shall add unto him the plagues that are written in this book. And if any man shall take away from the words of the book of this prophecy, God shall take away his part out of the book of life, and out of the holy city, and from the things which are written in this book."

This warning given by the Holy Spirit applies to the whole scripture. It is a serious matter to tamper with the word of truth. When the truth is tampered with, it distorts right conception of the work of redemption or Salvation. To preach false doctrine is wicked, just as any other sin is wicked. It is important and valuable before God and heaven to rightly instruct God's people and maintain a proper Christian faith by diligently searching and meditating on the scripture and not to proclaim false doctirines as truth.

The state of man

Other books by the author

1. The Quick Sands.
2. The Neme Boy & Doula - *Hard to Believe*, Volume 1
3. The Throne - *Hard to Believe*, Volume 2
4. David Lulu
5. The Third Eye

The state of man

INTRODUCTION

Varied beliefs and misconceptions abound concerning *the state of man*. Some say that a person does not really die. Death to them means, a transition to another world called a spiritual world. They believe that the soul of man is immortal or conscious at death. Some stretch this doctrines to believe that the soul undergoes a series of reincarnations. How true is this? If this theory of the soul undergoing a series of reincarnations is true, it will be incorrect to speak of human beings as actually dying. A lot of people also believe that the soul of a person goes to face the judgement of God immediately after death. It means that the righteous and the unrighteous soul goes immediately to heaven or hell after death. If this belief is true, it means there is no hope of resurrection of the dead and that Christ rising from the dead should not be given a serious thought. What about spiritualism- the act of communication of the living with the dead. How true is this? Does the living really communicate with the dead?

A diligent search of the scripture will help us as we try to understand the true nature of man. Certain events happened in the past. These events contributed immensely to promoting misconceptions on the true nature of man.

To begin with, it is pertinent to point out that it is a mistake to suppose that idolatry grew gradually through the unenlightenment of human thinking. It rose so suddenly being conceived with an intention to rebel. It was the birth of a cruel or tyrannical ambition at war with God's commands. It came into being to oppose the will and true worship of the known true God. It was to satisfy the lust of the flesh, the lust of the eyes, and the pride of life in the place of the Creator. It's author in the present dispensation, that is the generation after Noah, was Nimrod.

Nimrod was the grandson of Ham. The Bible says, "he began to be mighty in the earth." He was described "as a mighty hunter before the Lord".From all intimation, he was a mighty rebel, in fact, the mightiest rebel before the Lord. He was a hunter of the sons of men, urging them to leave the judgement of SHEM AND NOAH and adhere to the judgement of Nimrod. Babel or Babylon was the beginning of his kingdom. Babel was in the land of Shinar, where inhabitants of the earth (after the destruction of the world of Noah), who were as yet of one language and one speech, journeyed together from the east, under the leadership of Nimrod. He was the heaven-defying founder of a new system of rule and worship. He instituted a government by brute force and earthly wisdom and policy, and a religion, which kept aside the true God and set man to the adoration of the sun, moon and stars, impersonated in himself.

After this Nimrodic era, the world and its history egregiously progressed into another period called 'great

21

intellectual darkness'. This was a time when millions of saints were mercilessly killed for their unshakable faith in the truth, the gospel of Christ. That church of the dark ages that was prophesied about and which reigned supreme for one thousand, two hundred and sixty years and that trumpeted her lordly commands into the ears of listening Christendom, and flaunted her flamboyant banners before gaping crowds, were not the church of Christ, it was the body of "mystery of iniquity". It was a time of great "falling away".

The church then was filled with corruption, impurity and superstition. The church of the dark ages was merged with the state and used the machineryof the state to inflict gruesome punishment on the genuine Christians for failure to conform to obnoxious false doctrines. After the killing of the Saints, the Word of God and the knowledge of the truth was taken away from the people. In place of truth, fables and idolatrous traditions of man subtly mixed to suplant and alloy the true word of God. The soul consciousness at death; communication of the living with the dead, worship of God through angels (fallen) and so on, were among the objectionable doctrines brought into the church.

Evidently, God had a plan to restore His WORD- the gospel of truth and bring relief to his persecuted people. By His wisdom He raised the reformers who opposed the errors of the state church. As the word of God inspired by the Holy Ghost, was made available in the form of the Bible,

22

people began to understand the truth. The powers of that state church and the errors it portrays was broken.

Yet, this period of liberty to know the truth was once again subtly beclouded by a period called 'great
intellectual light'. This was a time when the eyes of many have become dazzled or dazed by the glare of human speculations 'science falsely so called,' 1Timothy 6:20.

It is pertinent once again to point out here, that God created man in his own image and endowed him with reasoning faculty or intellectual powers. These intellectual powers given to man should be held as a gift from his maker and should be employed in the service of truth and righteousness. But the problem here with the gift God gave man is that in the face of it, man forgot God, cherished pride and ambition and exalted their theories, fables, and traditions above the eternal WORD of God. This accounts for evolutionary philosophy, organized atheism in the form of liberalism, occultism and anti-genesis movement which have been unfortunately capturing the minds of so many everywhere.

Thus, this period of intellectual light has as well achieved greater harm to the word of God as the time of wickedness and ignorance of the truth when man wallowed in strange doctrines in the name of the Bible truth.

For instance, through science, mankind has been given another evolution to man contrary to the truth of the Bible. The scriptural origin of

23

man says, "God created man
in His own image, in the image of God created he him: male and female created he them", Genesis 1:27. "And the LORD God formed man of the dust of the ground, and breathed into his nostrils, the breath of life and man became a living soul", Genesis 2:7.

To say that man evolved from an animal a creature lower than man, is to disclaim the genesis truth of the Bible regarding man's creation. Just as the knowledge of the state of man as instructed by the scripture has been so much affected by pagan philosophy taking its stem from the period of intellectual darkness when error reigned instead of truth, and period of intellectual light when science and 'human reason' was upheld as the solution to man's problem instead of the WORD of God.

Therefore, varied beliefs abound about the state of man.

The scripture tells us, "Be not deceived: evil communications corrupt good manners. Awake to righteousness, and sin not; for some have not the knowledge of God: I speak this to your shame," I Corinthians 15:33,34.

The state of man

Chapter 1

HOW DID DEATH COME ABOUT?

Most times, the burial of a dead person, attracts great respect. This however differs depending on the status or position, wealth and personality or popularity of the deceased, their relatives, friends, neighbours, religion, social club or society and so on.

This pomp and circumstance accompanying the dead is most often believed to be creating peace, love, joy, happiness and general satisfaction to the bereaved person. It is also aimed at creating or attracting prestige and satisfaction for the owners and friends of the dead body. When these glamorous ceremonies and obsequies are done, the dead can now rest in peace and the living can now be content at having accorded a "worthy burial", to the deceased.

Strangely, many dead are buried with material possessions such as money, silver and gold, and other valuable items. These items might have been demanded or requested, as a dying wish by the dead. Even when the bereaved did not make any request, some of the living deem it fit to bury their loved ones with these material possessions.

Mysteriously, in some customs and traditions, burials
attract rituals and this involves the diabolic murder of some unfortunate human beings. The heads

25

of these people murdered are then buried along with this 'very important' bereaved title holder. Burial with human heads according to some traditional demands is aimed at appeasing the gods. It is also aimed at providing freedom and protection for the revered 'title holder'. This is understood to mean that as the titled man is guarded and revered here in the land of the living, so also, he should be treated in the land of the dead believed to be a conscious world.

Needless to say, these practices of glorifying and honouring the dead are undertaken because people lack knowledge of the true state of man.

The question now is, what is death and how did it come about?

Death simply means to lose one's life. It means to be without life. A person who is dead does not physically or bodily move about. He is not conscious. He cannot remember anything.

Job 14:21, speaking on the state of man says, "his sons come to honour, and he knowth it not; and they are brought low, but he perceiveth it not of them." Job understood death, to mean, complete unconsciousness.

What happens to this dead person? Solomon tells us.

"Then shall the dust return to the earth as it was". Ecclesiastes 12:7 (first part). Solomon understood that the dust which returns to the earth is the human body. In other words, the dead body is buried in the earth.

From the account of the Bible, death came

The state of man

as a result of man's disobedience. God created man in his own image. He put man in the Garden called Eden. Man's duty in this garden was to "dress and to keep it".

Man was created perfect. Death was not meant for man. Man was under specific instruction at the Garden of Eden:

"But of the tree of knowledge of good and evil, thou shall not eat of it; for in the day thou eateth thereof thou shall surely die", Genesis 2:17.

Already, Lucifer who later became the devil having forsook his allegiance to God was cast out of heaven. He was cast out with one third of the angels in heaven. They came down to the earth with wrath. His sole aim was to deceive and to lure man away from his creator. He desired followership among man, just as he was able to woo one third of the angels in heaven. He therefore devised a plan to get man to follow him. And he said unto the woman, "Yea, hath God said ye shall not eat of every tree of the garden?". Genesis 3:1.

The subtle beautiful serpent was the medium through whom Eve's attention was attracted. On further pressure by the serpent who said,"ye shall not surely die", Genesis 3:4 (last part), Eve had to desire the fruit and by this covetousness, she was drawn away by her own lust and enticed. So, she obeyed the serpent:

"And when the woman saw that the tree was good for food, and that it was pleasant to the eyes and a tree to be desired to make one wise, she took of the fruit thereof and did eat and gave also, unto her husband with her and he did eat," Genesis 3:6.

The issue here, is that, had Eve resisted the serpent, she would not have fallen to the temptation of Satan. She hearkened to the voice of Satan and then desired against the better instruction and judgement of her creator. If we desire something that is not ours, the odds are high that one day we will reach out and take it. We should always be on the side of our creator by listening and obeying him. The Bible advises us to:

"Submit yourselves to God. Resist the devil, and he will flee from you," James 4:7.

However, by this disobedience of Adam and Eve, their offspring were made sinners. David acknowledged this sinful nature when he said:

"Behold I was shapen in iniquity and in sin did my mother conceive me", Psalm 51:5.

Adam and Eve first died spiritually. The Spirit of God was no more striving with their own spirit because of sin. Their communion with God was affected. They were no longer confident before God.

Adam and Eve also died physically. Since then, death began to reign:

"Wherefore as by one man sin entered into the world and death by sin and so death passed upon all, for that all have sinned," Romans 5:12.

Clearly, it is sin that brought death.

The state of man

Chapter 2

WHERE DO THE DEAD GO?

What happens to a person when he dies? Where does he go?

Job pondered over this question and reasoned:

"For there is hope of a tree, if it be cut down, that it will sprout again, and that the tender branch thereof will not cease. Though the roots thereof wax old in the earth, and the stocks thereof die in the ground. Yet, through the scent of water it will bud, and bring forth boughs like a plant. But man dieth, and wasteth away; yea, man giveth up the ghost, and where is he?" Job.14: 7-10.

A retrospect on the origin of man will help our understanding as we answer this question:

"And the LORD God formed man out of the dust of the ground and breathed into his nostrils the breath of life; and man became a living soul," Genesis 2:7.

Looking deep into this scripture, it is clear here, that the man who was formed out of the ground had no life. But when God breathed into his nostrils, life came. What happened is that, immediately this breath was administered by God unto man, the brain leaped into action, the heart began to beat and blood flowed through man's veins. Thus, consciousness was produced. It is important to note here that this consciousness was not only due to the dust of the ground or the

29

human body. Neither is it only because of the breath of life. But the union of the breath of life with the dust of the ground or the human body, produced this consciousness.

Something happens when there is a reverse or break in this process. Solomon tells us:

"Then shall the dust (the body) return to the earth as it was; and the spirit shall return unto God who gave it", Ecclessiastes 12:7.

God is the source of life. Both the righteous and the wicked owe their life to God. The spirit is the link or source of consciousness. When there is a reverse in the process of living, the spirit given by God goes back to Him. This means, the breath which is the life principal is withdrawn and the body dissolves into dust from where it was made. The heart stops functioning or beating. The brain does not leap into action any more. The blood no longer flows through the veins. Man's consciousness is gone. In other words, the person is dead.

Job understood the source of man's consciousness when he said:

"All the while my breath is in me and the spirit of God is in my nostrils," Job 27:3.

"Thou hidest thy face, they are troubled: thou takest their **breath** they die and return to their dust: thou sendest forth thy spirit, they are created..." Psalm 104:29,30.

Elihu, also speaking from the uprightness of his heart said, "the spirit of God hath made me and the breath of the Almighty hath given me life,"

The state of man

Job 33:4.

"Thus said the LORD GOD unto these bones: behold, I will cause breath to enter into you, and you shall live", Ezekiel 37:5.

The spirit (breath) is the point of consciousness. It links the body (dust) and the soul to produce life or consciousness. From creation, it is clear that with the body alone, there is no life, but when the breath was administered, life came. In other words the spirit is the touch that magnetizes and lightens the body, thus, giving it consciousness or life. "For as the body without the spirit is dead. James 2:26.

A dead person does not know anything. His intelligence, love, good and bad thoughts end the moment the breath goes away. "His **breath** goeth forth, he returneth to his earth; in that very day his thoughts perish", Psalm 146:4.

"For the living know that they shall die: but the dead knows not anything: Neither have they any more a reward: for the memory of them is forgotten". Ecclesiastes 9:5.

The grace, mercy, faithfulness, love, peace, joy, miracles, blessings and power of God can only be experienced and appreciated by the living. It is only the living that can acknowledge Him in praise and true worship. The dead cannot. David, therefore declares:

"The dead praise not the LORD, neither any that go down into silence", Psalm 115:17.

"For in death, there is no remembrance of thee; in the grave who shall give thee thanks", Psalm 6:5

31

"Wilt thou show wonders to the dead? Shall the dead arise and praise thee? Shall thy loving kindness be declared in the grave? Or thy faithfulness in destruction? Shall thy wonders be known in the dark? And thy righteousness in the land of forgetfulness?", Psalm 88:10-12

King Hezekiah was sick unto death and a prophecy came from God through Isaiah that he the king was going to die. This wise king came to understand that only the living can praise God. He explored God's mercy and prayed fervently. "For the grave cannot praise thee, death cannot celebrate thee; they that go down into the pit cannot hope for thy truth. The living, he shall praise thee, as I do this day," Isaiah 38: 18-19.

Of course, God in His infinite mercy, who hearkens to the prayers of the righteous answered and commuted the death penalty to more healthy years for the king.

"For the living know that they shall die; but the dead know not anything, neither have they anymore reward? For the memory of them is forgotten. Also, their love and their hatred and their envy, is now perished; neither have they anymore portion forever in anything that is done under the sun". Ecclesiastes 9:5-6.

The living partakes of the activities of life. They can love, hate and be loved or hated. They can offer reward and be rewarded. But as soon as they die, they cannot be reckoned anymore among the living.

"Marvel not at this; for the hour is coming in which all that are in the graves shall hear his

32   *The state of man*

voice, and shall come forth; they that have done good, unto the resurrection of life; and they that have done evil, unto the resurrection of damnation", John 5:28-29.

It is clear that Job understood this message of our Lord Jesus Christ. He already said. "If I wait, the grave is mine home: I have made my bed in the darkness," Job 17:13.

The condition of man is that he is said to be asleep in the grave. "But I would not have you to be ignorant, brethren, concerning them which are asleep, that they sorrow not, even as others which have no hope". 1 Thessalonians 4:13.

Lazarus was raised from the dead after four days. Our Lord Jesus Christ did not call him from heaven or hell. He used the term "sleep" and "death" interchangeably. He did not tell us that Lazarus went to heaven or hell. He only spoke , "and when he thus had spoken, he cried with a loud voice: "*Lazarus come forth*", John 11:43.

On the day of Pentecost, Peter boldly declared as regards the state of the partriach David:

"Men and brethren, let me freely speak unto you of the partriach David, that he is both dead and buried, and his sepulchre is with us unto this day…for David is not ascended into the heavens; but he said himself. The Lord said unto my Lord, sit thou on my right hand, until I make thy foes thy footstool," Acts 2:29, 34-35.

By this sermon, Peter who was wholly taken over by the Spirit of God is saying that David had not gone to heaven at his death, but was

33

resting in his grave, waiting for the time when the power of death and grave shall be destroyed by Christ coming to take his own.

David himself declared: "As for me, I will behold thy face in righteousness: I shall be satisfied, when I awake, with thy likeness." Psalm 17:15.

"Then cometh the end when he shall have delivered up the kingdom to God even the Father, when He shall have put down all rule and all authority and power. The last enemy that shall be destroyed is death." 1 Corinthians 15:24, 26.

Job no doubt, had hope of living again:

"As the waters fail from the sea, and the flood decayeth and drieth up; so man lieth down, and riseth not: till the heavens be no more, they shall not awake, nor be raised out of their sleep. O that thou wouldest hide me in the grave, that thou wouldest keep me secret, until thy wrath be past, and that thou wouldest appoint me a set time, and remember me, if a man die, shall he live again? All the days of mine appointed time will I wait, till my change come. Thou shall call, and I will answer thee: thou will have a desire to the work of thine hands," Job 14:11-15.

The Grave remains the home of the dead until resurrection. Resurrection is the only hope of escape from the grave.

Chapter 3

THE SOUL

The popular belief is that the soul is without a body and that it is the immortal part of the human body. That it has reasoning faculty and that it can see, hear, love, and hate. It recollects past events and predicts future events. They believe that the soul leaves the body at death.

Some teach that the soul comes back to life through reincarnations. Others believe that the soul goes to face the judgement of God immediately after death. This means, that the soul of the righteous and the unrighteous dead are already in heaven or hell.

The Bible views and definitions of the soul are varied. In some senses, the Bible speaks of the soul as the life of the individual. In other senses, it refers to the soul as the living person or the mind of a person. The soul may mean, the affection or love of an individual, the dead body of a person, or the spirit of man. There is nowhere the Bible talks about the soul as an entity or personality that lives immortally apart from the body.

"And the LORD formed man from the dust of the ground, and breathed into his nostrils the breath of life; and man became a living soul." Genesis 2:7. The soul here refers to the entire person.

It must be categorically noted that it was

the union of the breath of life (as administered by God) and the dust (human body) of the ground that produced the first living person. Man became conscious as soon as this breath was administered to man by God.

God gave man a mind that could reason and comprehend:

"And Adam gave names to all cattle, and to the fowl of the air and to every beast of the field", Genesis 2:20 (first part). This reasoning and comprehensive ability that God gave man was not given to animals.

Man was beautifully made, formed by the hand of God, while animals were created by the word of God. Thus, David declared:

"I will praise thee; for I am fearfully made; marvelous are thy works; and that my soul knoweth right well." Psalm 139:14.

A man that has no mind cannot understand and know right. The mind of a human being knows right. "Therefore shall ye lay up those my words in your heart and in your soul, and bind them for a sign upon your hand, that they may be as frontlets between your eyes," Deuteronomy 11:18.

What the soul is capable of doing is innumerable as mentioned in the Bible. These are however, the functions of the mind.

The soul is an able director of man's actions:

"My soul hath kept thy testimonies; and I love them exceedingly", Psalm 119:167. In this text the soul is seen as the agent of obedience.

The soul takes counsel:

The state of man

" How long shall I take counsel in my soul having sorrow in my heart daily? how long shall my enemy be exalted over me ?", Psalm 13: 2.

The soul can refuse things:

"The things that my soul refused to touch are as my sorrowful meat", Job 6:7.

The soul can be grieved. "Did not I weep for thee that was in trouble? Was not my soul grieved for the poor?" Job 30:25.

The soul also feels the bitterness of sorrow:

"My soul is weary of my life: I will leave my complaint upon myself; I will speak in the bitterness of my soul", Job 10:1

Our Lord Jesus Christ at a time felt this sorrow of the soul when He was about to be offered us for mankind:

"And he taketh with him Peter and James and John, and began to be sore amazed, and to be very heavy: And said unto them, my soul is exceedingly sorrowful unto death; tarry ye here and watch". Mark 14:33,34.

The soul can be satisfied with good things:

"My soul shall be satisfied as with marrow and fatness: and my mouth shall praise thee with joyful lips". Psalm 63:5

The soul can die. "Behold, all souls are mine; as the soul of the father, so also, the soul of the son is mine. The soul that sinneth, it shall die", Ezekiel 18:4.

The soul can be saved from death:

"Let him know that he that converted the sinner from the error of his ways shall save a soul from death and shall hide multitude of sins".

The state of man

James 5: 20.

In the case of Abel who was killed by his brother Cain God did not say that the soul of Abel came to heaven to report. Rather, He said:

"The voice of thy brother's blood cried unto me from the ground", Genesis 4:10.

There is no where in the scripture where we are told that the soul of Adam and Eve lived on. To say that Adam was an immortal soul that could not die, only goes to defend satan and his lies which he told them in the Garden of Eden. And the serpent said unto the woman:

"Ye shall not surely die", Genesis 3:4 . The scripture records that, " And all the days that Adam lived was nine hundred and thirty years and he died.", Genesis 5:5.

Also, the people during Noah's time died for the sin they committed. The Bible records that:

"All in whose nostrils was the breath of life, died", Genesis 7:21 –23. No mention was made as to where their souls went.

A living human being can be led or controlled by either the Spirit of God or the spirit of the devil. Those who are led by the Spirit of God are called children of God:

" For as many as are led by the Spirit of God, are the Sons of God", Romans 8:14. They are usually taken over by the Holy Ghost.

The Holy Spirit or the Spirit of God or the Spirit of Christ is a distinct personality and part of the Godhead of Trinity. The work of the Holy Spirit is of the utmost importance to man. He is the immediate source of life:

The state of man

" But there is a spirit in man: and the inspiration of the Almighty giveth that spirit understanding." Job 32:8. "Thou hidest thy face, they are troubled: Thou takest their breath they die and return to their dust. Thou sendest forth thy Spirit, they are created..." Psalm 104:29, 30.

"The Spirit of God hath made me, and breath of the Almighty hath given me life," Job 33:4.

"Then said Jesus to them again, peace be unto you; as my Father hath sent me, even so send I you. And when he had said this, he breathed on them, and said unto them,
receive ye the Holy Ghost." John 20:21-22

The Holy Spirit played a part in the coming of our Lord and Saviour Jesus Christ Luke1: 35. He is the revealer of divine truth and the source of inspired scriptures, 11 Timothy 3:16.

This means the Holy Ghost is active in the conversion and edification of the believer by the word of which He is the author. As a result, the Holy Spirit is said to dwell in the heart of the believer, Romans 8:9.

The Spirit of God from time to time reveals things unto people. It could be either in visions or dreams, Daniel 2:29.

The scripture says, "For the prophecy came not in old time by the will of man but holy men of God spake as they were moved by the Holy Ghost", 2 Peter 1:21.

Ezekiel 2:2 says, "And the Spirit entered into me when he spoke unto me, and set me upon my feet that I heard him that spake unto me.

39

"Then the spirit took me up, and I heard behind me a voice of a great rushing, saying, blessed be the Glory of the **LORD** from his place. The spirit entered into me, and set me upon my feet, and spake with me, and said unto me"... Ezekiel 3:12, 24.

"And the Holy Ghost descended in a bodily shape like a dove upon him (Jesus), and a voice came from heaven which said, Thou art my beloved son; In thee I am well pleased". Luke 3 :22

"And when the day of Pentecost was fully come, they were all with one accord in one place. And suddenly there came a sound from heaven as of a rushing mighty wind, and it filled the room and there appeared unto them cloven tongue as of fire, and it sat upon each of them, and they were all filled with other tongues, as the Spirit gave them utterance", Acts 2 :1-4.

"I was in the Spirit on the Lord's day, and heard behind me a great voice, as of a trumpet," Rev. 10:1.

"And he carried me away in the Spirit to a great and high mountain, and showed me the great city, the holy Jerusalem descending out of heaven from God".Rev 21:10

" But he (Stephen), being filled with the Holy Ghost, looked up steadfastly into heaven, and saw the glory of God", Acts 7:5.

"And when they were come up out of the water, the Spirit of the Lord caught away Philip, that the eunuch saw him no more and he went his way", Acts 8:39.

The state of man

"As many as receiveth him (Christ) to them he giveth power (Holy Spirit) to become sons of God even to them that call upon his Name", John 1:12.

"But ye shall receive power after the Holy Ghost is come upon you," Acts 8:1.

From these scriptures, it is clear that the Spirit of God takes hold of the mind (the soul) or the spirit and gives revelation knowledge. The Holy Spirit can therefore, give visions of things to come, just as John was given the Book of Revelation, which contains the revelation of things to come (given during John's time).

By this Revelation, man was given the opportunity to glimpse into heaven to discover so many things concerning the worship of the eternal God. The Spirit can also give a person visions of heaven or hell to teach the living the reality of such conditions. Many have been shown these visions and several other visions. These visions does not in any way cancel the truth of the state of man as the scripture holds it.

In the same vein, those who are led by the devil are usually possessed by the evil spirit. As such, they also receive revelations and manifest the character of the devil.

"Know ye not that to whom ye yield yourselves servants, his servant ye are to whom ye obey, whether of sin unto death or of obedience unto righteousness," Romans 16:16

The devil is a deceiver. He is the supreme

41

spirit of evil. He has deceived so many people. For instance, in the Garden of Eden, he was able to deceive Adam and Eve on immortality for them even if they disobeyed God by going contrary to His instruction. This of course, resulted in death for man, Genesis 3: 4,5.

The devil is the ruler of a kingdom which has powers. He is the god and prince of the world (the world which opposes God) and goes about seeking to devour and enslave men.

Instances abound in the scripture where many have yielded themselves to the influence of satan.

"Then entered satan into Judas surnamed Iscariot of the number of the twelve", Luke 22:2. The result was that he was able to betray his master.

"Peter said to them (Ananias and Saphira), why hath satan filled your heart to lie to the Holy Ghost." … Acts 5:3,4. Of course, this couple died for lying against the Holy Ghost.

"But shun profane and vain babblings for they will increase unto more ungodliness. And their word will eat as doth a canker, of whom is hymaneous and philetus; who concerning the truth have erred, saying that the resurrection is past already and overthrew the faith of some", 2 Timothy 2;16,18. Those people were found guilty of heresies. They subverted the word of God. There are still so many today who are doing the same thing.

"And when the woman saw that the tree

The state of man

was good for food, and that it was pleasant to the eyes, and a tree to be DESIRED to make one wise, she took of the fruit thereof and did eat, and gave also unto her husband with her; and he did eat", Genesis 3:6. The consequences of this covetousness was that death came to reign.

Witches and wizards, necromancers, mystics or occult societies, false religions, apostate and spiritual churches, false prophets, and so on are under the influence of the devil. They have been possessed or taken over by the devil. The result is that all kinds of deception and strange doctrines such as soul consciousness at death; communication with the spirit of the dead and so on abound.

The understanding given man by God was not taken away from man after he sinned. What God did was to send man out of the Garden of Eden, so that man will not eat of the tree of life and live forever in sin. Man was given freedom of choice. He could choose good or bad. The consolation is that goodness awaits man's choice of good. While evil and damnation awaits his choice of evil.

The offspring of Adam and Eve were henceforth conceived in sin:

"Behold, I was shapen in iniquity; and in sin did my mother conceived me", Psalm 51:5.

It was God's plan to deliver man from the hand of the devil. It is God's plan that all men should be saved. This is why God sent His Son into the world that we might come to His saving knowledge by living the life of His Son, Jesus

The state of man

Christ.

When a person is converted or receives Christ, the spirit of such a person becomes the dwelling place of God. The spirit of such a person is alive unto God. " And you hath he quickened who were dead in trespasses and sin." Ephesians 2:1.

For the quickened human spirit empowered by the Holy Spirit to control the soul (mind) of man and the soul in turn control the body, the person needs to be in a helpless condition. He needs to be incapable of doing things for himself in the strength of the soul and the body. In other words, he has whole-heartedly turned to God. This means that the human spirit controlled and empowered by the Holy Spirit will take control and lead the whole man God's way in every way. This brings us to sanctification. "And the very God of peace sanctify you wholly; and I pray God your whole spirit and soul and body be preserved blameless unto the coming of our Lord Jesus Christ", I Thessalonians 5:23.

Here, Paul combines the three to emphasize that no part of man should be shut out of the experience of sanctification.

When this happens, the person can be said to be mature in the Lord. He is among the sons of God. "As many as are lead by the Spirit of God they are the sons of God."

Man is whole and complete. The Bible does not speak of a conscious entity able to live or exist apart from man.

44

SOURCE OF IMMORTALITY

Immortality belongs only to God. This also establishes the truth that mankind does not have immortality:

"I give thee charge in the sight of God, who quickeneth all things, and before Christ Jesus, who before Pontius Pilate witnessed a good confession, that thou keep this commandment without spot, unrebukeable, until the appearing of our Lord Jesus Christ; which in his time he shall shew, who is the blessed and only potentate, the king of kings, and Lord of Lords, who only hath immortality, dwelling in the light which no man can approach unto, who no man hath seen, nor can see; to whom be honour and power everlasting. Amen", I Timothy 6:13-16.

Man in his sinful condition is spiritually dead. He also awaits the physical death at the appointed time. The wrath of God is also awaiting him and the dangers of eternal death:

"But after thy hardness and impenitent heart treasureth up unto thyself wrath against the day of wrath and revelation of the righteous judgment of God, who will render to every man according to his deeds; to them who by patient continuance in well doing seek for glory and honour and immortality, life eternal," Romans 2:5-7.

But after the grace of God abundantly appeared through the merits of our Lord Jesus Christ, we can be saved from the wrath of God. We could also, be saved from eternal death:

"But is now made manifest by the

45

appearing of our Saviour Jesus Christ, who hath abolished death, and hath ***brought life and immortality to light through the gospel". 2Timothy 1: 10. Man can therefore, receive immortality or eternal life through acceptance of the gospel.***

When a person accepts the gospel, he expects to be given or to receive immortality during the day of rapture. "Behold, I shew you a mystery; we shall not all sleep. But we shall all be changed, in a moment, in the twinkling of an eye, at the last triumph; for the trumpet shall sound, and we shall all be changed. For this corruptible, shall have put on incorruption and this mortal shall have put on immortality, then shall be brought to pass the saying that is written, death is swallowed up in victory", I Corinthians 15:54-55.

It was the devil that first taught and deceived man on immortality for man when he told Eve, "thou shall not surely die", Our Lord Jesus Christ rightly described the devil as "the father of all lies", John 8:44.

The state of man

Chapter 4

SPIRITUALISM

The act of the living communicating with the dead is called Spiritualism. How true is this concept?.

Spiritualism is not really a Biblical term. Adherents to this belief accept the natural immortality of man as basic. It would be incorrect to speak of a person dying if the lines of communication are forever open between the living and the dead. The dividing line between the living and the dead is in relation to knowledge, ***"for the living know that they shall die, but the dead knows not anything",*** Ecclesiastes 9:5.

Who is the first spirit medium? Genesis 3:1, "Now the serpent was more subtle than any beast of the field which the LORD God had made. And he said unto the woman, yea, hath God said, ye shall not eat of every tree of the garden".

The serpent who beguiled Eve through his subtlety was the first spirit medium. Since that day the result of every medium contact has been to deceive. The devil was able to gain control of the serpent. From all outward appearances it was the serpent speaking and Eve thought she was really
talking with the serpent when in truth she was talking with the devil himself.

Revelation 12:9 referred to the devil as

47

"that old serpent, called the devil and satan which deceiveth the whole world".

The serpent basically told Eve "ye shall not surely die" Genesis 3:4. He was able to get Adam and Eve to act in opposition to God's truth. It was this lie that brought death to man. And hence Jesus Christ referred to the devil as "a murderer from the beginning, and abode not in the truth, because there is no truth in him; for when he speaketh a lie, he speaketh of his own; he is a liar and the father of it all". John 8:44.

Satan carries out this delusion through his fallen angels who do his bidding. These fallen angels appear as messengers from the spirit world. While professing to bring the living into communication with the dead, the prince of evil exercises his bewitching influence upon their minds. The appearance of those who died could be brought by satan before those who go to seek after them. The replica of the person, look, word, tone of voice and so on are reproduced with exactness. These are called familiar spirits. Familiar spirits are those diving demons present in the physical body of the conjurer. When it is therefore, believed that the dead actually return to communicate with the living, satan causes those familiar spirits to appear. They take the form of those who had been dead and buried. Having assumed this posture, they make all kinds of claims. They could reveal secrets, foretell and predict events. They also offer certain solutions.

The Bible is against spiritualism. The scripture categorically declares, that **"the dead**

The state of man

knows not anything".

God condemns and forbids all purported communication with familiar spirits:

"There shall not be found among you anyone that maketh his son or his daughter to pass through the fire, or that useth divination, or an observer of times, or an enchanter or a witch, or a charmer, or a consulter with familiar spirits, or a wizard, or a necrommancer, for all that do those things are an abomination unto the Lord: and because of these abominations the Lord thy God doth drive them out from before thee", Deuteronomy 18:10-12.

"And the soul that turneth after such as have familiar spirits, and after wizards to go a whoring after them, I will even set my face against that soul, and will cut him off from among his people. A man also or woman that hath a familiar spirit, or that is a wizard, shall surely be put to death. They shall stone them with stones: their blood shall be upon them",
Leviticus 20:6, 27.

In those days in Israel both spirit medium and those who consult them were put to death. Israel was a special nation originally chosen by God - a nation in whose shores should not be found spiritualism or any other form of idolatory. Already, the nations that were set by God for occupation by Israel were helplessly caught up in these abominations. This was the reason God set them out for destruction and
occupation by Israel. Israel did occupy the land as promised by God. Yet most often they

49

disobeyed by finding themselves also in these abominations. "They joined themselves also unto Baal-poer and ate the sacrifices of the dead"; Psalm 106:28.

Of course, the anger of God was released on them: "And the LORD said unto Moses, take all the heads of the people, and hang them up before the LORD, against the sun that the fierce anger of the LORD may be turned away on Israel. And Moses said unto the judges of Israel; Slay ye everyone his man that were joined unto Baal-poer" , Numbers 25:4.

When Saul was king over Israel, he did not spare those with spirit mediums. They were put to death and out of the land. But when he disobeyed God and was at the point of frustration and discomfort from God, he went to seek counsel with the witch of Endor and inquired not of the Lord.

"And when Saul inquired of the Lord, the Lord answered him not neither by dreams, nor by Urim, nor by prophets. Then said Saul unto his servants. Seek me a woman that hath a familiar spirit that I may go to her and inquire of her. And his servants said to him behold, there is a woman that hath a familiar spirit at Endor", 1Samuel 28:6, 7.

But Saul died "for his transgressions and for asking counsel of one that had a familiar spirit, to inquire of it," 1Chronicles 10:13 (last part).

"But I say that the things which the Gentiles sacrifice, they sacrifice to the devils, and not to God and I would not that ye should have fellowship with devils", 1 Corinthians 10:20. Paul advises against any contact, even by food offered in sacrifice to hearthen gods.

Spiritualism has led to diverse and strange doctrines aimed at undermining the truth of God. The result of this falsehood is that no difference is drawn between the righteous and the unrighteous dead. The reason that the so-called spirit of the dead state some truth in their claims, gives them credibility and acceptance, and so a great multitude go a whoring after them. The Bible is then interpreted to please the carnal unrenewed hearts, while its salient truth is rendered ineffective. Little or no difference is drawn between good and evil. Rather, God as a symbol of love is dwelt upon and this is exploited to deceive. Thus, God's hatred of sin and punishment of offenders; obedience to his holy laws; faith in Christ; constant reading and meditation on the scriptures, are swept aside or vaguely taught. These people indeed "have the form of godliness but deny the power thereof".

Paul declares that before the Second Coming of our Lord Jesus Christ, there will be manifestation of satanic power:

"Now the spirit speaketh expressly, that in the latter times some shall depart from the faith, giving heed to seducing spirits and doctrines of devils. 1Timothy 4:1. The supernatural manifestations of these spirits implement this deception giving them plausibility.

Certainly, the coming of Christ is to be preceded by satanic doctrines. "Even him whose

The state of man

coming is after the working of Satan with all power and signs and lying wonders. And with all deceivableness of unrighteousness in them that perish; because they received not the love of the truth they might be saved" 2 Thessalonians 2:9-10.Those who constantly reject the Bible truth will be deceived.

To avoid being ensnared, "when they shall say unto you, seek unto them that have familiar spirits, and unto wizards that peep, and that mutter; should not a people seek unto their God, for the living to the dead; to the law and to the testimony; if they speak not according to this *Word,* it is because there is no light in them", Isaiah 19:20. If only the living can simply hearken to the truth in the Bible regarding the nature of man, they would see falsehood of satan, his power and lies in spiritualism.

Those who will stand the days of trials must read, understand and quote with faith and power the scriptures to repulse the devil's intrigues. We must be steadfast to overcome the "hour of temptation".

These visitants will tend to appeal to people's deepest sympathies and even work miracles to sustain their deception. Those whose faith is not deeply established on the word of God will be deceived and overcome. Satan is working with "all deceiveableness of unrighteousness" to gain control of people. His temptation is daily on the increase. Those who are sincerely seeking knowledge of truth of the Bible and really living according to this precept, will find in Christ a sure

52

protection. They have "kept the word of his patience".

The devil has released delusions through organized paganism, atheism, humanism, evolutionary philosophy and the anti-genesis movement and also through the error of 'false sciences' to undermine faith in the scripture. Also, delusions are emanating from so many religions, apostate Christian bodies, to conflict the truth of the gospel. This is aimed at making all united with the devil in his last great stand against God and His children. Beware! These "mysteries of iniquity" which have been at work are being subtly intensified at this end time "for the mystery of iniquity doth already work: only he who letteth will let, until he be taken out of the way", 2Thessalonians 2:7.

Finally, the death of man is the creation of man in reverse. Man was made out of the dust. He was not conscious until God breathed into him and life came.

When death comes, man's "breath goeth forth", he ceases to think. He cannot move. He is totally unconscious. "His body returns to the earth from whence it came".

"Consider and hear me oh my God; lighten mine eyes, lest I sleep the sleep of death," Psalm 13:3.

Until resurrection there is no communication between the dead and the living.

The state of man

Chapter 5

RESURRECTION

Resurrection means the rising of the dead at a latter day. From the earliest times the hope of resurrection has been the belief of man. There will be no future life without resurrection. Job, from the earliest time understood this when he said:

"If a man die, shall he live again? All the days of my appointed time will I wait, till my change come. Thou shall call, and I will answer thee: thou shall have a desire to the work of thine hands," Job 14:14,15.

Job also, recognised that the hope of resurrection depended on Christs' return to the earth the second time. "For I know that my **Redeemer** liveth, and that he shall stand at the latter day, upon the earth: and though after my skin worms destroy this body, yet in my flesh shall I see God: whom I shall see for myself, and mine eyes shall behold, and not another, though my reins be consumed within me", Job 19:25-27.

David speaking by the Spirit expects to have God's likeness.

"As for me, I will behold thy face in righteousness: I shall be satisfied, when I awake, with thy likeness", Psalm 17:15.He expects "To be partaker of God's divine nature having escaped the corruption that is in this world through lust", (11 Peter 1:4).

In the time of Jesus, the doctrine of

The state of man

resurrection was well established among the Jews, though it was denied by the Sadducees. Some came to Him the same day saying: "That there is no resurrection and asked Him, saying, Master, Moses said, if a man die, having no children, his brother shall marry his wife, and raise up seed unto his brother. Now there are with us seven brethren, and the first, when he married a wife, deceased, and having no issue, left his wife unto his brother: likewise the second also, and the third unto the seventh. And last of all the woman died also. Therefore in the resurrection whose wife shall she be of the seven? For they all had her. Jesus answered and said unto them. Ye do err, not knowing the scripture, nor the power of God. For in the resurrection they neither marry, nor are given in marriage, but are as the angels of God in heaven. But as touching the resurrection of the dead, have ye not read that which was spoken unto you by God saying I am the God of Abraham, and the God of Isaac and the God of Jacob? God is not the God of the dead but of the living," Matthew 22:23-32.

God is the God of the living and so Jesus promised the sleeping saints:

" And thou shall be recompensed at the resurrection of the just:", Luke 14:14.

There was also controversy as Paul reasoned:

"And when they heard of resurrection of the dead, some mocked: and others said, we will hear thee again of this matter," Acts 17:32.

Resurrection is important. It is the basis of

The state of man

Christianity. Without it, there will be no Christianity. Paul asked, " Now if Christ be preached that He rose from the dead, how say some among you that there is no resurrection of the dead? But if there be no resurrection of the dead, then is Christ not risen: and if Christ be not risen, then is our preaching vain, and your faith is also vain. Yea, and we are found false witnesses of God; because we have testified of God that he raised up Christ: whom he raised not up, if so be that the dead rise not, for if the dead rise not, then is not Christ raised, your faith is vain, ye are yet in your sins. Then, they also which are fallen asleep in Christ are perished. If in this life only we have hope in Christ, we are of all man most miserable", 1 Corinthians 15:12-19.

The hope of the believers is resurrection and this is based on the fact that Christ is risen or resurrected. The resurrection of our Lord Jesus Christ and that of the believers in him are linked together. The most important event to have ever taken place is the resurrection of Christ.

Truly, the believer's hope of resurrection is Jesus: "And Jesus said unto her, I am the resurrection and the life: he that believeth in me, though he were dead, yet shall he live: and whosoever liveth and believeth in me shall never die", John 11:25,26.

In Revelation 1:18, Jesus also declared:

"I am he that liveth, and was dead, and behold, I am alive for evermore, Amen; and have the keys of hell and of death." The mystery of Godliness was complete in Christ, who manifested in the flesh, preached unto us, suffered for our sakes, died, buried and resurrected for our justification and also, an indication that we should partake of his resurrection.

"But now is Christ risen from the dead and became the first fruit of them that rose from the dead," 1 Corinthians 15:20. Thus, Jesus who came in the flesh, became the first among the flesh and blood to rise from the dead.

Many people believe that the sinner, after he passes from this life, have another chance to be saved. They believe sinners go to a spirit world at death, and there the gospel is preached to them. Now, how was the gospel preached to the dead?

" **For for** this cause was the **gospel preached also to them that are dead**, that they might be judged according to men in the flesh, but live according to God in the spirit", 1 Peter 4:6.

When this verse is hurriedly read, it gives the impression that the gospel was preached to the dead. This text is saying "for this cause was the gospel preached (in the past) also, to them that are (in the present) dead". Those people to whom the gospel was preached were alive but they are now dead. It is not possible to preach to the dead in the light of what the scripture says about   them," the dead knows nothing", Ecclesiastes 9:5.

How did Christ preach to the Spirits in prison:

"By which he went and preached unto the

spirits in prison; which sometimes were disobedient, when once the longsuffering of God waited in the days of Noah, while the ark was a preparing wherein few, that is eight souls were saved by water", 1 Peter 3:11,20.

What Peter is saying here is that Christ preached to the people who were before the flood in Noah's day. They were in the prison house of sin. By the Holy Spirit through Noah's Ministry the provision made available at the Calvary was made available to those people before the flood. "For the grace that bringeth salvation has appeared to all men ", Titus 2:11. No other provision has ever been made for man to escape from the devils prison house. " There is no other name given under heaven whereby man can be saved except that name Jesus Christ", Acts 4:12. Redemption is through " the precious Blood of Christ, as a Lamb without blemish and without spot, who verily was foreordained before the foundation of the world, but was manifest in these last times for you", 1 Peter 1:10, 20.

The Holy Spirit which is also, the Spirit of Christ has been at work for man right from the beginning. Paul mentioned:

" And did all drink the same spiritual drink: For they drank of that Spiritual Rock that followed them: And that Rock was Christ. Neither let us tempt Christ, as some of them tempted, and were destroyed of serpents", 1 Corinthians 10:1-9.

So the scripture did not say that Christ preached in person to the spirits in prison. The Bible does not speak of the concept of

The state of man

disembodied spirit. He preached by the Holy Spirit through the ministry of Noah.

"And sparred not the old world, but saved Noah the eight person, a preacher of righteousness, bringing in the flood upon the world of the ungodly." 11 Peter 2:5. So those spirits in prison refers to living men and women. The scripture never meant prison to be hell or a lake of fire. Isaiah prophesied about Christ's ministry, "I the LORD have called thee in righteousness, and will hold thine hand, and will keep thee, and give thee for a covenant of the people, for a light of the Gentiles; to open the blind eyes, to bring out the prisoners from the *prison,* and them that sit in darkness out of the prison house," Isaiah 42:6,7. ***It is the gospel that looses people from prison the house of sin.***

Also, Peter speaking by the Spirit referred to what David earlier said, "He David seeing this before spake of the resurrection of Christ that his soul was not left in hell," Acts 2:3. Christ was not left in the grave. He is risen. The scripture does not teach that Jesus went into a place of torment at death.

Jesus on the cross at the point of death said... "Father, into thy hands I commend my Spirit... and having said thus, he give up the ghost", Luke 23:46.

The scripture teaches that Christ arose and triumphed over death:

"Ye men of Israel, hear these words, Jesus of Nazareth, a man approved of God among you by miracles and wonders and signs, which God

The state of man

did by him in the midst of you, as ye yourselves also know: him, being delivered by the determinate counsel and fore-knowledge of God, ye have taken, and by wicked hands have crucified and slain: whom God hath raised up, having loosed the pains of death: because it was not possible that he should be holden of it. This Jesus hath God raised up, whereof we are all witnesses", Acts 2:22-24, 32.

Jesus has promised those who love him and serve him, "Because I live, ye shall also live", John 14:19.

The scripture also condemned the wrong practice of those who baptise the dead. "Else what shall they do which are baptised for the dead, if the dead rise not at all? Why are they baptised for the dead", 1 Corinthians 15:29,

There is no possibility of salvation after death. One must personally accept Christ, repent and confess his sins, in order to profit by baptism and be saved. Death brings a close to human probation.

There is certainty of resurrection. And no second chance of salvation after death:

" For as in Adam all die, even so in Christ shall all be made alive. But every man in his own order: Christ the firstfruits; afterward they that are Christ's at his coming. Then cometh the end, when he shall have delivered up the kingdom to God even the father; when he shall have put down all rule and all authority and power," 1 Corinthians 15:22-25.

Paul had implicit confidence and hope of

The state of man

resurrection. He desired:

"If by any means I might attain unto the resurrection of the dead", Philippians 3:11.

The account of the rich man and Lazarus is another passage of the scripture widely and aptly adduced to support the doctrine of immortality for man. Some take the account to be a literal history of two men. Others feel it is a fiction used as a parable. In both, the account is used to prove two doctrines: that man is conscious between death and the resurrection, and that men go to their reward or punishment immediately after death.

"And it came to pass, that the beggar died and was carried by the angels into Abraham's bosom: the rich man also died and was buried: And in hell he lifted up his eyes being in torment, and seeth Abraham afar off and Lazarus in his bosom. And he cried and said, father Abraham have mercy on me and send Lazarus, that he may dip the tip of his finger in water and cool my tongue for I am tormented in this flame", Luke 16:22-24.

From this text some people hold on to the natural immortality of the soul by venturing to answer that it was not the real bodily Lazarus but rather his soul. Here, there is no mention of the soul of the rich man and Lazarus.

The meaning of this parable has no reference to the condition of man between death and resurrection. This parable has something to do with the murmuring of the Jews "saying this man (Jesus) receiveth sinners, and eateth with them", Luke 15:2.

Jesus never denied this charge. He justified His actions by introducing this parable as well as others, such as the parable of the lost sheep, Luke 15:3-7;parable of the lost piece of money, Luke 15:8-10; parable of the Prodigal son, Luke 15:11-32; parable of the unjust steward, Luke 16:1-13.

Just as in other parables, Christ gave the parable of the rich man and Lazarus to teach important truths through their preconceived opinions – as the doctrine of a conscious state of existence between death and the resurrection was held by man at that time. Christ met people on their own ground.

This parable teaches us that;

(a) Man determine his destiny in this life, as vividly portrayed by the agonies of the unrighteous wicked man who lived in affluence and denied the truth of God by not helping the poor. What you will sow here is what you will reap here and afterwards.

(b) The probation period is ended by death. "And he cried and said, father Abraham, have mercy on me and send Lazarus, that he may deep the tip of his finger in water, and cool my tongue, for I am tormented in this flame", Luke 16:22-24. It is not possible for a dead man, particularly in torment to come back and preach the gospel to the living.

(c) Man creates a gulf between himself and God by his own choice. In this parable also is a contrast between the wealthy who do not place their trust in God and the poor who had trusted

The state of man

God.

The wall of partition between Jews and Gentiles had been broken down by Christ's coming.

" For he is our peace, who hath made both one, and hath broken down the middle wall of partition between us," Ephesians 2:14. He came that we may have equal opportunity for salvation. And so this parable has no reference to a future punishment and condition of man between death and the resurrection. The doctrine of immortality of the soul is not supported by the Bible. The only way to obtain life in another world after death is by resurrection.

The account of the repentant thief is another scriptural passage most often quoted to prove man's immortality and that man goes to his reward at death:

"And he said unto Jesus, Lord, remember me when thou comest into thy Kingdom. And Jesus said unto him, verily I say unto thee, today shall thou be with me in paradise", Luke 23:42-43.

The question to be answered here is whether Christ promised the thief that he would be with him that day in paradise or did he simply tell him that that day he was giving him the assurance of salvation. The Bible answer to the remaining questions in this study will tell us what Christ meant. The adverb today, is between two clauses, which in the Greek means " truly to you I say, and with me you will be in paradise". The New Testament was earlier preserved in Greek

The state of man

and there was no punctuation until later in the fifteenth and sixteenth centuries. This was during the reformation. It was during this time that punctuation was introduced.

However, subsequent development, particularly, on the day of crucifixion, will open our eyes more:

"This man (Joseph, counsellor, a good and just man) went unto Pilate, and begged the body of Jesus. And he took it down, and wrapped it in Linen, and wherein never man before was laid", Luke 23:52,53. Christ did not go to His father in heaven the day he died. He only commended His Spirit unto God. For three days after His resurrection Jesus said to Mary:

"Touch me not; for I am not yet ascended to my father: but go to my brethren, and say unto them, I ascend unto my father and your father; and to my God, and your God", John 20:17.

To say that the thief went to heaven on the crucifixion day and to use this to support the immortality of man is not the right way to interpret the Bible to make the text the foundation of doctrine which contradicts other plain scriptures on the subject. It is also clear that the repentant thief did not die on the day of his crucifixion:

"The Jews therefore, because it was the preparation that the bodies should not remain upon the cross on the Sabbath day (for that Sabbath day was an high day) besought Pilate that their leg might be broken and that they might be taken away. Then came the soldiers, and brake the legs of the first, and of the other, which was

64

crucified with Him. But when they came to Jesus, and saw that He was dead already, they brake not His legs", John 19:31-33.

There is only one way to have eternal life after the resurrection and live forever:

"He that believeth on the son hath everlasting life. And he that believeth not the son shall not see life; but the wrath of God abideth on him", John 3:36.

Two resurrection are mentioned by our Lord Jesus Christ – the resurrection of the righteous or just and the resurrection of the unrighteous or the wicked.

" Marvel not at this: for the hour is coming, in the which all that are in the graves shall hear his voice, and shall come forth; they that have done good, unto the resurrection of life; and they that have done evil, unto the resurrection of damnation", John 5:28,29.

WHAT BODY DO THE DEAD RISE?

"But some man will say, How are the dead raised up? and with what body do they come?" I Corinthians 15:35.

The scripture tells us the kind of bodies the righteous will have at resurrection:

"For our conversation is in heaven: from whence also we look for the Saviour, the Lord Jesus Christ: who shall change our vile body, that it may be fashioned like unto his glorious body, according to the working whereby he is able to subdue all things unto himself." Philippians 3:20,21.

The state of man

This particular scripture is better understood in detail, in I Corinthians 15:36-55:

"Thou fool, that which thou sowest is not quickened, except it die: And that which thou sowest, thou sowest not that body that shall be, but bare grain, it may chance of wheat, or of some other grain: But God giveth it a body as it hath pleased him, and to every seed his own body. All flesh is not the same flesh: but there is one kind of flesh of men, another flesh of beasts, another of fishes and another of birds. There are also celestial bodies, and bodies terrestrial: but the glory of the celestial is one, and the glory of the terrestrial is another. There is one glory of the sun, and another glory of the moon, and another glory of the stars: for one star differeth from another star in glory. So also is the resurrection of the dead: it is sown in corruption; it is raised in incorruption: it is sown in dishonour; it is raised in glory: it is sown in weakness; it is raised in power: it is sown a natural body; it is raised a spiritual body. There is a natural body, and there is a spiritual body. And so it is written, the first man Adam was made a living soul; the last Adam was made a quickening spirit. Howbeit that was not first which is spiritual, but that which is natural; and afterward that which is spiritual. The first man is of the earth, earthy. The second man is the Lord from heaven. As is the earthy, such are they also that are earthy: and as it is heavenly, such are they also,that are heavenly. And as we have borne the image of the earthy, we shall also bear the image of the heavenly. Now this I say,

The state of man

Brethren, that flesh and blood cannot inherit the kingdom of God; neither doth corruption inherit incorruption. Behold, I shew you a mystery; we shall not all sleep, but we shall all be changed, in a moment, in the twinkling of an eye, at the last trump: for the trumpet shall sound and the dead shall be raised incoruptible, and we shall be changed. For this corruptible *must* put on incorruption, and this mortal *must* put on immortality. So when this corruptible shall have put on incorruption, and this mortal shall have put on immortality, then shall be brought to pass the saying that is written, Death is swallowed up in victory. O death where is thy sting? O grave, where is thy victory"

Resurrection of the dead is compared to that of seed which when planted first decays and then springs forth a new life. It is spectacular that the righteous are raised up in incorruption. This means that the natural vile body that was dead and buried rises up a new spiritual and glorious body like that of the Lord Jesus Christ at his resurrection. And it is only those who have been quickened from trespasses or sins (Ephesians 2) and who walked in the spirit of Christ and become sons of God or children of God and fellow heirs and joint heirs with Christ, who can partake of this glorious resurrection (Romans 8:11). Those who walked in the flesh and have not the spirit of Christ (Romans 8:9; I Corinthians 15:47-50) cannot take part in this glorious resurrection.

It is obvious that the bodies of the righteous at resurrection will be glorious like unto the glorious body of our Lord and Saviour Jesus Christ. The scripture made it clear that we shall be like him:

"Beloved, now are we the sons of God, and it doth not yet appear what we shall be: but we know that, when he shall appear, we shall **be like him**; for we shall see him as he is," I John 3:2.

Our Lord Jesus Christ had a real body after He passed through death. There are three positive proofs to the fact that he had a real body after he was resurrected. Firstly, the disciples could see Him. Secondly, they could touch Him. Thirdly, He ate food before them. He was not in form of spirit. He had bones and real tangible body, Luke 24:36-43.

When Jesus spoke and called "Mary", she quickly recognised her master's voice, John 20:11-16.

The disciples of Jesus Christ also, recognised Him by His appearance. He looked the same. Every imperfection disappeared. All the pains and agonies inflicted upon Him disappeared, John 20:19,20, 26-29.

Jesus was also made known in breaking of bread. It was His natural habit to raise His hands as He blessed the food, Luke 24:13-35.

Just as Christ was recognised after having passed through death the righteous can expect the same kind of recognition. All imperfection will disappear but this will not do away with the personal identity:

"For as the new heavens and the new earth, which I will make, shall remain before me,

The state of man

saith the LORD, so shall your seed and your name remain," Isaiah 66:22.

The righteous will also know many in heaven they have not met on earth. This could be understood from the recognition of Moses and Elijah on the mount of transfiguration, Mark 9:2-5. Peter, James and John had never met Moses and Elijah before, but they were able to recognise them. This simply shows that the righteous shall know people even better than they know them here on earth.

The righteous indeed shall have real tangible bodies, Romans 8:23. The resurrection of the righteous is indeed going to be glorious. "*For the earnest expectation of the creature waiteth for the manifestation of the sons of God*," Romans 8:19.

"And this is the will of Him that sent me, that everyone which seeth the Son, and believeth on Him, may have everlasting life: and I will raise him up at the last day," John 6:40.

"But thanks be to God, which giveth us the victory through our Lord Jesus Christ. Therefore, my beloved brethren, be ye steadfast, immovable, always abounding in the work of the Lord, for as much as ye know that your labour is not in vain in the Lord," I Corinthians 15:57,58.

THE FIRST RESURRECTION

The resurrection of the righteous is called the first resurrection:

"For this we say unto you by the word of the Lord, that we which are alive and remain unto

69

the coming of the Lord shall not prevent them which are asleep. For the Lord himself shall descend from heaven with a shout, with the voice of the archangel, and with the trump of God: and **the dead in Christ shall rise first.** Then, we which are alive and remain shall be caught up with them in the clouds, to meet the Lord", 1 Thessalonians 4:15-17.

This first resurrection is otherwise called the **Rapture of the church.** This resurrection pictures the righteous of all ages alive and reigning with Christ for a thousand years:
"And I saw thrones, and they that sat upon them: and I saw the souls of those that were beheaded for the witness of Jesus, and for the word of God, and which had not worshipped the beast, neither his image, neither had received his mark upon their foreheads, or in their hands; and they lived and reigned with Christ a thousand years. The rest of the dead lived not again until the thousand years were finished. This is the first resurrection – Blessed and holy is he that hath part in the first resurrection on such the second death hath no power, but they shall be priests of God and of Christ and shall reign with him a thousand years", Revelation 20:4-6.

Note, that, what John was given was a vision of the things that must come to pass. So, the souls mentioned here should not in any way cause confusion as there is no immortality or disembodiment of the soul. This rapture of the church takes place during the Second Coming of our Lord Jesus Christ, as He promised, that he

The state of man

will come again and receive us unto himself, John 14:12,3.

The one thousand years reign is otherwise called the millennium. Some have the idea that the millennium will be a thousand years of peace and prosperity on the earth. This is very erroneous and against the scripture. This wrong teaching is a handout from satan to deceive.

During this one thousand years, the saints with Christ in heaven engage in judgement over the wicked. This judgement by the righteous is part of God's plan to vindicate Himself in His dealing with the wicked. God does not want to leave anyone in doubt as to His work on behalf of man. So, for the one thousand years, the righteous will critically examine the record of the wicked. They will discover that the punishment to be given to the wicked by the just God is deserved, since they will learn of every effort made to proclaim the gospel to everyone for salvation.

While the saints are in heaven for this one thousand years, satan will be imprisoned upon the earth:

"And I saw an angel come down from heaven, having the key of the bottomless pit and a great chain in his hands. And he laid hold on the dragon, that old serpent which is the devil, and satan, and bound him a thousand years. And cast him into the bottomless pit and shut him up, and set a seal upon him, that he should deceive the nations no more, till the thousand years should be fulfilled: and after that he must be loosed a little season", Revelation 20:1-3.

71

This key mentioned here is significant in our understanding of the angel and his action towards satan. Isaiah predicted of Christ:

" And the key of the house of David will I lay upon his shoulder. So he shall open, and no man shall shut and shut no man shall open", Isaiah 22:22.

Also, John wrote:

"And to the angel of the church of Philadelphia write: these things said he that is holy, he that is true, he that openeth the key of David, he that openeth, and no man shutteth; and shutteth, and no man openeth", Revelation 3:7.

Satan will not escape from this bottomless pit. The term "bottomless pit", comes from the Greek word abuses from which we get abyss. This means that everything will be in a state of chaos. This "bottomless pit" is a chain of circumstance by which the devil and his angels are bound. They are restricted to the dilapidated earth as no access for them is given to the other world of the righteous with Christ. Satan is wholly cut off from his deception which for centuries he has been caught up with. During this millennium, he wanders to and from the empty earth as his sins against the law of God, dawns on him. He looks forward to a dreadful future when he must pay for all his sinful acts. It is a terrible time for him and he suffers intensely.

Prior to this bottomless pit in which satan is to be kept, are some facts which mark the millennium.

The earth is made desolate:

The state of man

"Behold the LORD maketh the earth empty and maketh it waste, and turneth it upside down, and scattereth abroad the inhabitants thereof. The land shall be utterly empty and utterly spoiled: For the LORD hath spoken this", Isaiah 24:1,3:

"I beheld the earth, and lo, it was without form and void; and the heavens, and they had no light. I beheld the mountains and lo, they trembled and all the hills moved lightly. I beheld and lo, there was no man, and all the birds of heaven were fled. I beheld and lo, the fruitful place was a wilderness, and all the cities thereof were broken at the presence of the Lord and by his fierce anger", Jeremaiah 4:23-26.

These helpless conditions will be brought about after Christ comes to take his own during the rapture. The plagues recorded in Revelation 16, will help to bring about this desolate situation. Therefore, "the bottomless pit" refers to these conditions – the righteous are gone to heaven; the wicked are all dead; there is no one for the devil to tempt to sin for one thousand years. The earth will be completely ruined and depopulated.

SECOND RESURRECTION

The close of the millennium brings us to the second resurrection. The terrible plagues unleashed on the earth after the rapture of the saints will not allow any of the wicked to live until the one thousand years have expired. Satan *"must be loosed for a little season."* This liberty is for short duration:

73

"And when the thousand years are expired, Satan shall be loosed out of the prison. And shall go out to deceive the nations which are in the four quarters of the earth, gog and Magog, to gather the nations together to battle: the number of whom is as the sand of the sea. And they went up on the breath of the earth, and compassed the camp of the saints about, and the beloved city (New Jerusalem)", Revelation 20:7-8.

At the end of this one thousand years, certain events will cause the loosing of Satan to his final work of deception.

LOOKING INTO THE NEW JERUSALEM

Before we go into the event that will cause the loosing of satan, it is interesting and pertinent for us to cast a view through the revelation given to John. God by His grace gave us the privilege to glimpse into heaven to discover the activities involved in the worship of the eternal God. We are also given the privilege to catch a glimpse of the New Jerusalem in its eternal beauty. It is necessary for us to look at it and ponder over its beauty since it is going to be the home of the redeemed or the saints after the rapture of the church. This new Jerusalem also holds a lot of attraction to the devil and the host of his agents.

The human mind cannot adequately comprehend the reality and beauty of those things God has prepared for those who love Him. Our

74

brother Paul noted this when he was speaking to the people of Corinthians:

"Eye hath not seen, nor ear heard, neither have entered into the heart of man, the things which God hath prepared for them that love Him," 1Corithians 2:9.

On this basis the future world that we have every right to expect based upon God's promises, can but vaguely be comprehended now.

This New Jerusalem which descends from God will be a factual city. It will be really beautiful. It is referred to as "the bride, the lamb's wife", not only on account of the sanctified buildings, structures, and avenues arranged in some fixed shapes for the accommodation of the inhabitants. The New Jerusalem appears in her eternal form and completeness. The detailed description of the living and the inanimate occupants and beings is given in the book of revelation:

"Having the glory of God: and her light was like unto a stone most precious, even like a jasper stone, clear as crystal; And had a wall great and high, and had twelve gates, and at the gates twelve angels, and names written thereon, which are the names of the twelve tribes of children of Israel: On the east three gates; on the north three gates; on the South three gates; and on the West three gates. And the wall of the city had twelve foundations, and in them the names of the twelve apostles of the Lamb. And he that talked with me had a golden reed to measure the city, and the gates thereof, and the wall thereof. And the city lieth foursquare, and the length is as large as the

The state of man

breath: and he measured the city with the reed, twelve thousand furlongs. The length and the breath and the height of it are equal. And he measured the wall thereof, an hundred and forty and four cubics, according to the measure of a man, that, of the angel. And the building of the wall of it was of jasper: and the city was pure gold, like unto clear glass. And the foundations of the wall of the city were garnished with all manners of precious stones. The first foundation was jasper; the second, sapphire; the third, a chalcedony. The fourth, an emerald; the fifth, sardonyx; the sixth, sardius; the seventh, chrysolite; the eighth, beryl; the ninth, a topaz; the tenth, a chrysoprasus; the eleventh, a jacinth; the twelfth, an amethyst. And the twelve gates were twelve pearls; every several gate was of one pearl; and the street of the city was pure gold, as it was transparent glass. And I saw no temple therein: for the Lord God Almighty and the LORD are the temple of it. And the city had no need of the sun, neither of the moon, to shine in it! For the glory of God did lighten it, and the Lamb is the light thereof", Revelation 21:11-23

This description reveals that what we see in the New Jerusalem is the glory of God and the Lamb only. Of course, the throne of God and the Lamb will be there. Created light like the sun and the moon cannot shine in the presence of the Creator and the city having the glory of God. The predominating colour of the light here, is that of jasper. This Jasper is a beautiful sea green, very clear like that of a diamond.

76

Everlasting memorial is given to each of the twelve tribes of Israel in the New Jerusalem since their names are inscribed on the city's gates. So, also are the twelve apostles of Jesus Christ whose names are inscribed on the foundations of the city. At each gate was a guiding angel. John saw one of the angels take a golden read and measure the city. The city was found to be equal on each side with circumference of 12,000 furlongs. Since eight furlongs make a mile it means the New Jerusalem is 375 miles on each side, making a total of 1500 miles in circumference. The measurement of the walls were 144 Cubits which is 18 feet in height using 18 inches to a cubit. The height of the city is said to be equal to the length and to the breath. This means the city would be in the form of a perfect cube. The walls are of jasper while the city itself is said to be pure gold. This gold has the transparency of glass. This is a great display of the righteousness of God.

Its twelve foundations are constructed of precious stones. One can give a lot of imaginative interpretation to the various colours of the stones. At the base is the jasper, which is typical of the suffering and death of the Saviour slain from the foundation of the world. Above it, is the sapphire, like a blue flame of truth. The white chalcedony reflects the purity of Christ's life. While the emerald, which is bright green in colour is like the rainbow about the throne, and gives hope to others who rest upon it. The sardonyx reflects many colours but above it is the deep red sardius

77

covered by the Chrysolite. Above this is the beautiful beryl whose light mingles with blazing topaz to tell the story of joy and peace in the Lord. The jacinth with violent colour is the purple of royalty. This is crowned with the purity of the red rose amethyst. This city is perfect. It has never been seen before. It indeed challenges our imagination.

Each of the twelve gates had a pearl. Pearl, is a precious substance which is found inside the shell of mollusks. Jesus and his message was called " The Pearl of Great Price (Matthew 13:46)", showing its great value to man. In this New Jerusalem, there will be no temple where God meets with His people. The saints will be in God's presence. They will have full and free access to both God and the Lamb. The people of God are privileged to hold open communion with the Father and the Son. This means that the anticipated fellowship with God since the fall of man will be restored. Faith will give way to sight.

"And the nations of them which are saved shall walk in the light of it; and the Kings of the earth do bring their glory and honour into it. And the gates shall not be shut at all day: for there shall be no night there. And they shall bring the glory and honour of the nations into it", Revelations 21:24.

This is saying that those inside this New Jerusalem are children of God and nations in the New earth.

"And I saw a new heaven and a new earth: for the first heaven and the first earth were passed

The state of man

away," Revelation 21 :1.

All will be certainly sanctified and holy. They will happily worship the only true and Living God. It has been stated that in the New Jerusalem, there will be no sun or moon or stars. But in the new earth, these heavenly bodies which God created to rule day and night will continue to shine on earth outside the New Jerusalem. With regard to the sun and the moon in the new earth, the prophecy of Isaiah says: "Moreover the light of the moon shall be as the light of the sun, and the light of the sun shall be seven-fold", Isaiah 30:26.

John gave further description of the new Jerusalem. "And he showed me a pure river of water of life, clear as crystal, proceeding out of the throne of God and of the Lamb. In the midst of the street of it, and on either side of the river, was there the tree of life, which bore twelve manner of fruits, and yielded her fruit every month: and the leaves of the tree were for the healing of the nations. And there shall be no more curse: but the throne of God and of the Lamb shall be in it; and his servants shall serve him: And they shall see his face: and his name shall be in their foreheads", Revelation 22:1-4.

The New Jerusalem as further described by John has noticeable similarity to the description of the Garden of Eden recorded in genesis. In that Eden, there was a river with four branches which provided water for the garden, Genesis 2:10. In the New Jerusalem, the river of life is restored. David mentioned this river in Psalm 46:4:

"There is a river, the streams whereof shall

make glad the city of God, the holy place of the tabernacles of the Most High".

In this garden in the New Jerusalem, there is also, a tree of life, just as it was in the garden of Eden where Adam and Eve were before they sinned. Some information is given about this tree. The fruits of this tree had power to perpetuate life - it contains all the essential elements to perpetuate life-this tree which surpases in glory all other trees in the garden has a purpose to assure the saint's life without interruption. It should be noted that Adam and Eve had access to this tree until they sinned, as a result of which they were chased out of the garden home and angels were stationed at the tree of life so that sinful man should not eat its fruit and become immortal, Genesis 3:23,24.

Other beautiful trees of various kinds with fragrant and delicious fruits were in abundance in this garden. It should not be forgotten that the work of Adam and Eve in the garden of Eden was to "dress and keep" beautiful vines, by trimming the branches to form arbors, thus making for themselves a dwelling from the living trees covered with foliage and fruits. Delicate flowers rich in profusion greet the eyes at every turn. The air is clear and health giving. Everything is beautiful beyond description and wonderful.It is perfect.

In this garden, there will be "no more curse". This means perfect freedom from everything evil. The devil will no longer be able to tempt the inhabitants. Most wonderful is that

The state of man

the throne of God and of Christ will be there.

In this new dispensation the city home of the people of God will be the New Jerusalem while their country home will be somewhere in the new earth. The inhabitants of the earth will go to the New Jerusalem at least five times every month for two reasons: On each Sabbath, they will assemble to worship God at the New Jerusalem; when there is a new moon that is every twenty-eight days, they will also go to the New Jerusalem. Going to the holy city at every new moon could have a lot to do with the tree of life that bears its fruits at every new moon, since the fruit is for the saints and the nation. The Prophet Isaiah spoke about this visit in Isaiah 66:22,23:

"For as the new heavens and the earth, which I will make, shall remain before me, saith the LORD, so shall your seed and your name remain. And it shall come to pass, that from the one new moon to another, and from one Sabbath to another, shall all flesh come to worship before me", saith the LORD."

Also John mentions of a new heaven. The sky above our earth is the first heaven and is called the firmament heaven in Genesis 1:8,20. This heaven has been polluted by sin and therefore will be destroyed as stated in 2Peter 3:10-13:

"But the day of the Lord will come as a thief in the night; in which the heavens shall pass away with a great noise, and the elements shall melt with fervent heat, the earth also and the works that are therein shall be burned up.

The state of man

Nevertheless we, according to his promise look for a new heaven and new earth wherein dwelleth righteousness."

While the heavenly bodies (sun,moon, stars) are, called the second heaven which as you have heard shall pass away with the earth and all therein- the old shall be destroyed and the new brought into being. The heaven above the two is called paradise. Paul says:

"I know a man in Christ above fourteen years ago, whether in the body, I cannot tell or whether out of the body, I cannot tell: God knoweth: Such one caught up to the THIRD HEAVEN. How that he was caught up into paradise", 2 Corinthians 12: 3, 4.

Now, who are those to be inside the New Jerusalem and how can one be qualified? And who are those outside this new dispensation?

"Blessed are they that do his commandments, that they may have right to the tree of life, and may enter in through the gates into the city. For without are dogs, and sorcerers, and whoremongers and murderers, and idolaters, and whosoever loveth and maketh lie", Revelation 22:14,15.

Anyone, who wants to be part of the New Jerusalem and the new earth, will have his or her name registered in the lamb's book of life. This is a great opportunity and honour gracefully given to man and it calls for celebration. Jesus told his disciples who were rejoicing having successfully cast out demons from people:

"Notwithstanding in this rejoice not, that the

The state of man

spirits are subject unto you, rather rejoice, because your names are written in heaven," Luke 10:20.

For one to be qualified or have his name written in the book of life, one must have soberly decided to fellow Jesus. You must accept Christ as Saviour and Lord. You do not look back when you have taken this decision. It is a wise choice.

This book of life is made up of all who have diligently entered the service of God. Which means, they were sinners, but they have all truly repented of sin, by claiming the BLOOD of Christ as their atoning sacrifice. When they have by faith done this, they receive forgiveness entered against their names in the book of heaven. Having been pardoned, they become partakers of Christ righteousness and their characters are found to be in line with the Law of God. Their sins being blotted out completely upon total establishment in Christ, they will be accounted worthy of entry into the heavenly city, the New Jerusalem. This is tantamount to saying that their robes have been washed and made white in the blood of Jesus. John wanted to know and so one of the twenty - four elders in God's throne said to him.

"Who are these who are arranged in white robes? And whence came they? And (John) said unto him, sir, thou knowest. And he said to me, these are they which came out of great tribulation, and have washed their robes, and made them white in the blood of the Lamb", Revelation 7:13,14.

The washing of robes is absolutely

The state of man

essential to fellowship with Christ. Without Christ atoning His blood, their can be no fruit of obedience. Keeping of commandments without acceptance of the blood atonement does not grant eternal life:

"For by grace are ye saved, through faith and that not of yourselves it is the gift of God: Not of works, lest any man should boast. For we are his workmanship, created in Christ Jesus unto good works, which God hath before ordained that we should walk in them", Ephesians 2:8-10.

No matter how we try to keep the commandment, we cannot be saved if we have not accepted by faith Jesus Christ as Saviour, allowing Him to wash us from our sins with His own precious blood. The entire redeemed host will reach heaven because they have washed their robes and made them white in the blood of the Lamb. In other words they are wearing the righteousness of Christ.

But those on the outside who are not allowed into the New Jerusalem are:

"The fearful, and unbelieving, and the abominable, and murderers, and whoremongers, and sorcerers and idolaters and all liars", Revelation 21:8.

These are also, the same as those mentioned in Revelation 22:15.

These "fearful and unbelieving" ones are those who have failed to live up to expectation. They did not walk constantly in the righteousness of Christ. They give up easily. They are faithless. They do not completely trust God. They are not

The state of man

trustworthy. Also, on the outside are the" abominable", the workers of abominations and "murderers together with "whoremongers and sorcerers". These people commit their sins in secret, thinking that God does not know. They worship God with their mouths while their hearts go after their covetousness. They are like those our Lord Jesus Christ described in Matthew 23:27:

"Woe unto you, scribes and Pharisees, hypocrites! For ye are like unto whited sepulchres, which indeed appear beautiful outward, but within are full of dead men bones, and of all uncleanness".

Outside are the "idolaters and liars". These have no respect for God. They have no regrets about changing the truth of God into a lie. The Bible warns:

"For I testify unto every man that heareth the words of the prophecy of this book, if any man shall add unto these things, God shall take away his part out of the book of life, and out of the holy city, (New Jerusalem) and from the things which are written in this book," Revelation 22:18,19.

This warning applies to all the scriptures in the Bible. It is a serious matter to tamper with the word of truth. When truth is perverted this distorts the right conception of the work of redemption or salvation. To preach false doctrine is as wicked as any other sin. It is important and vital before God and heaven to rightly instruct God's people and maintain a proper Christian faith by diligently searching and meditating upon the scripture and not to proclaim false doctrines as truth.

So far with the visions and the beauty of the New Jerusalem and those that will be inside it.

Let us now cast our minds back to the events that will cause the loosing of satan at the end of the one thousand years.

The first event is the descending of the New Jerusalem with Christ and the saints inside it:

"And I John saw the holy city, New Jerusalem coming down from God out of heaven, prepared as a bride adorned for her husband." Revelation 21:2

The second event is the resurrection of all the wicked from all ages:

"But the rest of the dead lived not again until the thousand years were finished", Revelation 20:5

The wicked will not live until the thousand years be expired. They will be resurrected. Should you discover that a loved one is not in heaven during the millennium you can find the reason for this by looking over the records. God has given a thousand years to the judgement. It will be recognised by all that their punishment is deserved and that God is just.

The third event is that with the resurrection of the wicked, Satan now goes forth wildly in his mission of devastating delusion against nations. The term "Gog and Magog" is used to represent all the nations of the earth. Satan goes to them with a purpose of wooing them to overthrow the

The state of man

government of God and take possession of the New Jerusalem.

There have been several confederacies engendered by Satan against God and His people in the past, but this will be the last human confederacy against the Creator and His children. The devil and his angels and agents gather the kings of the earth, emperors, warriors, mighty men from all ages to come together against the New Jerusalem which has come down from above. When they look at the great number on their side, they consider themselves very confident to have captured the New Jerusalem. The army on the side of Satan would be such as was never convened by earthly conquerors – such as the combined forces of all ages since the history of war began on earth. This is called Armegeddon.

Thus, with all the sophisticated weapons of war, the host of the evil gathering, march on to death. Their punishment and overthrow is swift and final. They will be "devoured" by fire that God rains from heaven. And they were cast into a lake of fire. This is the second death. And death and hell were cast into the lake of fire", Revelation 20:14

Also, "the fearful and unbelieving, and the abominable, and murderers, and whore mongers, and sorcerers, and idolaters, and all liars shall have their part in the lake of fire which burneth with fire and brimstone which is the second death". Revelation 21:8.

"And I saw a great white throne, and he that sat on it, from whose face the earth and the

87

heaven fled away: and there was found no place for them. And I saw the dead, small and great stand before God! and the books were opened: and another book was opened, which is the book of life: and the dead were judged out of those things which were written in it: and death and hell delivered up the dead which were in them: and they were judged every man according to his works, and death and hell were thrown into the lake of fire. This is the second death. And whosoever was not found in the book of life was cast into the lake of fire", Revelation 20:11-20.

Here the Ancient of Days comes to execute sentence against the wicked. This is the last judgement sentence.

His throne which is described as white, symbolises perfect righteousness and justice. This characterises the Glory and Majesty of the eternal God. It should be noted that this is not the same type of investigative judgement in heaven which embraces the work of examination of characters, of determining who are prepared for the Kingdom of God - here, when the works of investigation shall be ended, when the cases of those who in all ages have professed to be followers of Christ have been examined and decided, probation will close:

"He that is unjust, let him be unjust still: and he that is filthy, let him be filthy: and he that is righteous, let him be righteous still: and he that is holy, let him be holy still", Revelation 22:11,12. Man's character has matured and the door of mercy will be shut. This investigative judgement

The state of man

is demonstrated in the parable of "the marriage feast" and "the ten virgins" in Matthew 22 and Matthew 25, respectively.

Also, the white throne judgement is not the same as the judgement of the wicked – the saints carefully examining the records of the wicked for one thousand years in heaven.

The white throne judgment has no need to go over the records of the wicked since the records have been carefully examined. This Great white throne judgement begins so that the judge of the universe can execute the final sentence against sin and sinners.

There is nobody whose life and history is not recorded in heaven. The basis of the judgement is the "works" or "deeds" done. When the book of life is opened, it will be discovered that the wicked did not avail themselves of Christ righteousness since their names were not found in any of the pages. They despised the gospel, neglected God's grace and mercy, rejected the atoning sacrifice of Jesus Christ for sin. They are sentenced as a result of these.

The government of God is justice. His punishment and sentence against the wicked is based upon the records of the sin they have unrepentantly committed:

"For God shall bring every work into judgement, with every secret thing, whether it be good, or whether it be evil", Ecclesiastes 12:14.

" But I say unto you that every word that man shall speak, they shall give account thereof in the day of judgement", Matthew 12:36.

The state of man

Further, God's justice is seen in the fact that He does not hurry when dealing with sin and sinners:

"The Lord is not slack concerning his promise, as some men count slackness, but is longsuffering to us- ward, not willing that any should perish, but that all should come to repentance", 2 Peter 3:9.

The wicked are not thrown immediately into the lake of fire until after their judgement during the one thousand years.

The state of man

FOR THE LIVING

Only the living can be instructed. "The dead knows not anything," Ecclesiastes 9:5

The Bible therefore, advises: **"WHATSOEVER THY HAND FINDETH TO DO, DO IT WITH THY MIGHT, FOR THERE IS NO WORK, NOR DEVICE, NOR KNOWLEDGE, NOR WISDOM IN THE GRAVE WHITHER THOU GOEST,"Ecclesiastes 9:10**
There is no work or activity and there is no wisdom or knowledge in the grave. While we live, we should wholly walk in Christ righteousness to glorify God. These are enumerated:
LOVE
"No man hath seen God at any time. If we love one another, God dwelleth in us, and his love is perfected in us", 1 John 4:12. Love is the all purpose of living. In loving, the living should love God with all his heart, soul,mind, body, strength and also, love his neighbour as himself.

The love of God is patient and kind. This love is enduring and rewarding. This is the love that holds the wrath of the Almighty God from being released upon sinners all over the world. Many, today, have deeply repented and are saved having availed themselves of the patience and kindness of our God. For the scripture says:

"The Lord is not slack concerning his

91

promise, as some men count slackness, but is **LONGSUFFERING** to us-ward, not willing that any should perish,but that all should come to repentance", 2 Peter 3:9

This simply explains that the delay of the judgement of God is for the benefit of mankind. His promise of bringing the world to judgement must be fulfilled. While many are availing themselves of His patience and kindness to repent, many are still despising the riches of His goodness by dismissing the judgement messages as illusion and refusing to repent.They ignorantly reason that the judgement message has been on for thousands of years and nothing has ever happened. But these people are unaware of one thing:

"That one day is with the Lord as a thousand years, and a thousand years as one day", 2 Peter 3:8.

The love that God has bestowed on us is unconditional and perfect. 1 John 4:10 Says. "Herein is love, not that we loved God, but that he loved us, and sent his son to be the propitiation for our sins".

The love of God which is in Christ Jesus is perfect. This love is patient, kind, enduring and fearless-the love that made Jesus Christ endure such contradiction of sinners and became obedient even unto the death on the cross for our redemption. Hence, the scripture urges us to:

"Look "unto Jesus the author and finisher of our faith: who for the joy that was set before him endured the cross, despising the shame, and

The state of man

is set down at the right hand of the throne of God", Hebrews12:2.

Christ in His human flesh was tempted as we are, yet He knew no sin. He suffered being touched with the feelings of our infirmities and by this He is able to give comfort to those who are tempted or who are persecuted. Of course, He did not endure or suffer in vain. He reaped the joy of His persecution and sufferings.
The scripture says:

"For it pleased the father that in him should all fulness dwell: And having made peace through the blood of his cross, by him to reconcile all things unto himself; by him, I say whether they be things in earth or things in heaven", Colossians 1:19,20.

Jesus Christ has truly reconciled us unto God and set us free from sin by His blood. Besides, Christ's name has been exalted above other names. All things in heaven and on earth bow at His name and all prayers ascend to God through Him.

The faithful in Christ looks unto Him since they too will be entitled to their crown of glory having endured persecutions:

"For I reckon that the sufferings of this present time are not worthy to be compared with the glory which shall be revealed in us", Romans 8:18.

The living must understand this love of God and live perfectly in it. This love eschews envy, hatred, bitterness and grudges; it is not easily made angry and it is not irritable or resentful; there is no selfishness and boastfulness

93

in this love; it does not rejoice in the misfortunes of others, instead, it rejoices in the truth; this love bears and believes all things.Therefore, we are instructed to:

"Owe no man anything, but love one another; for he that loveth another hath fulfilled the Law, love worketh no ill to his neighbours: therefore love is the fulfilling of the law, "Romans 13:8,10

Love is the perfection of the law. It is the only standard for measuring growth and maturity in Christianity. Says the scripture:

"When I was a child, I spake as a child. I understood as a child; but when I became a man, I put away childish things", 1 Corinthians 13:11.

All the gifts of God such as prophecy, knowledge, faith, speaking in tongues and so on are necessary, but they alone cannot make a man perfect. To have them is good because they edify the body of Christ. These gifts are just knowing in part. The perfection of all things is LOVE. The scripture describes he that has no love as " a sounding brass or a tinkling cymbal", 1 Corinthinas 13:1. This love brings us into divine relationship with God since "GOD IS LOVE," 1 John 4:8.

WISDOM

There is no wisdom or knowledge or understanding in the grave.

Only the living can exercise wisdom:

"And unto man He (GOD) said, behold, the fear of the Lord that is wisdom and to depart from evil, that is understanding", Job 28:28.

Knowledge is accumulation of the instruction of God. Wisdom is application of stored knowledge. Where there is absence of the knowledge of the word of God, things do not actually work out well. In such a state, problems are solved carnally. Some people could have the fear of God, that is, they know that there is God and that He should be feared and worshiped by attending service every Sunday yet, they have not the knowledge or the word of God. When such people are confronted with a matter, they become confused and hence resort to solving them carnally. The solution therefore, is in knowing the WORD and applying the word rightly to achieve good results -this is wisdom.

There is nothing our God does without applying wisdom. David declared:

"O LORD how manifold are thy works: in wisdom hast thou made them all: the earth is full of thy riches", Psalm 104:24. Daniel also declared, "Blessed be the name of God for ever and ever:for wisdom and might is his", Daniel 2:20.

Says wisdom, "The LORD possessed me in the beginning of his ways before his works of old; Proverbs 8:22.

God never created anything without His wisdom. Also, every problem is solved by His application of wisdom. Before the creation of Lucifer for instance, God by His unsearchable wisdom knew what this creature called Lucifer would turn out to be and He (God) predetermined to take care of it. How and what happened?

Before the foundation of the world, God

The state of man

had determined that redemption of man would be through the shedding of the Blood of His son Jesus Christ (for God knew the pollution and problems this Lucifer who later turned devil would constitute to His (God's) creatures, particularly, man who was to be created in God's own image). Therefore, these problems that were to affect His creation and creatures could only be purged through BLOOD. The scripture says:

"Almost all things are by the Law purged with blood: and without shedding of Blood is no remission", Hebrews 9:22.

Man is not redeemed with material things:

"Forasmuch as ye know that ye were not redeemed with corruptible things, as silver and gold from your vain conversation received by tradition from your fathers; but with the Precious Blood of Jesus Christ, as a lamb without blemish and without spot. Who verily was foreordained before the foundation of the world, but was manifest in these last times for you", 1 Peter 1:18-20.

This sacrifice, that is, the shedding of blood which was foreordained for man even before man's creation shows how important man is in the realm of creation.

The nature of what Lucifer would be who was to be created by God could be likened to the Bible references speaking about the wicked, in Isaiah 48:8:

"Yea thou heardest not: yea, thou knowest not:yea, from the time thine ear was not opened: for I know that thou wouldest deal very

96

treacherously, and wast called a transgressor from the womb."

Also, in Psalm 58:3:

"The wicked are estranged from the womb; They go astray as soon as they be born, speaking lies".

This means that Lucifer even before his creation had been known to become wicked, treacherous and even a murderer as Christ speaks of him:

"He was a murderer from the begining, and abode not in the truth, because there is no truth in him. When he speaketh a lie, he speaketh of his own: for he is a liar and the father of it", John 8:44.

This knowledge beforehand of the corrupt nature of Lucifer had been known by the wisdom of God. It is not in line with the will of God that Lucifer should sin. God is holy and His eyes cannot behold iniquity. Yet, He created him. God's creation and creature would know His wisdom to overcome. So Lucifer's sin is not by accident. Also salvation for mankind is not by accident.

Eventually, Lucifer was created. the Bible records concerning him:

"Thou was perfect in thy ways from the day that thou was created till iniquity was found in thee", Ezekiel 28:15.

Lucifer when created was so beautiful and was empowered. He was "in Eden the garden of God: every precious stone was thy covering. the sardius, topaz, and the diamond, the beryl, the onyx, and the jasper, the sapphire, the emerals,

The state of man

and the carbuncle, and gold: The workmanship of thy tabrets and of thy pipes was prepared in thee in the day that thou was created. thou art anointed cherub that covereth:and I have set thee so: thou was upon the holy mountain of God: thou hast walked up and down in the midst of the stones of fire", Ezekiel 28:13,14.

Thus, Lucifer was so adorned. He was one of the guardians of God's throne and he did his work in the throne room where he "walked up and down in the midst of the stones of fire". This is a representation of the glistering pavement of God's throne.

In the midst of Lucifers perfection sin was to be discovered. What was this sin?:

"Thine heart was lifted up because of thy beauty, thou hast corrupted thy wisdom by reason of thy beauty," Ezekiel 28:17

Lucifer became proud and coveted God's glory. He had an ambition to be exalted above God:

"For thou hast said in thine heart , I will ascend into heaven, I will exalt my throne above the stars of God. I will sit also upon the mount of the congregation, in the sides of the north: I will ascend above the heights of the clouds: I will be like the most High", Isaiah 14:13,14.

And so, a war broke out in heaven:

"Michael and his Angels fought against the dragon: and the dragon fought against his angels. And prevailed not: neither was their place found any more in heaven. And the great dragon (Lucifer) was cast out, that old serpent, which

The state of man

deceiveth the whole world: he was cast out into the earth, and his angels were cast out with him", Revelation 12:7-9.

Satan came down to the earth with wrath and resolved to make man who is created in the image of God to follow him. He successfuly schemed and tempted Adam and Eve. Hence sin came to the earth and increased.

But he (satan) never knew God's wisdom which was in Him from the beginning. God pronounced satan's punishment at the garden of Eden when he tempted man:

"And I will put enmity between thee and the woman and between thy seed and her seed: it shall bruise thy head and thou shall bruise his heel," Genesis 3:15.

When the fulness of time came therefore, God sent forth His WORD (Christ) to be born in the likeness of flesh to deliver His children from death and destruction of the devil.

Note, that Christ is that WORD (the wisdom) of God that brought light to darkness in the beginning as records in Genesis 1:1-3:

"In The beginning God created the heaven and the earth." In this first verse, there was no problem. But problems arose in the second verse because :the earth was without form, and void; and darkness was upon the face of the deep".Here, the earth was shapeless, empty and darkness all through. But the wise and powerful God who had the wisdom stored in Him applied it:

"And the Spirit of God moved upon the face

99

of the waters. And God said, "let there be light: and there was light".

The wisdom of God is light and it brings light to every darkness. Christ is the power and wisdon of God. 1 Corinthians 1:24:

"But unto them which are called both Jews and Greeks, **CHRIST THE POWER OF GOD AND THE WISDOM OF GOD".**

Christ is the light of the world. He has been with God from the beginning. Says the scripture:

"In the beginning was the WORD, and the word was with God, and the word was God. The same was in the beginning with God. All things were made by Him; and without Him was not anything made that was made. In him was life and the life was the LIGHT of men. And the light shinneth in darkness and the darkness comprehended it not. And the word was made flesh and dwelt among us (and we beheld his glory, the glory as of the only begotten of the Father) full of grace and truth", John 1:1-5,14.

The devil never knew this unsearchable wisdom of our God. And so, when His Son Jesus Christ was born by a virgin called Mary through the overpowering of the Holy Ghost, Satan was not happy, hence he sought to kill the child. To achieve his aim, satan entered into the heart of Herod to kill all the children under two years of age born in Bethlehem at that time, since the three wise men refused coming back to him (Herod) to relate their findings about the new born Christ the king. But God by His wisdom already instructed Joseph to take the young child and the

100

mother and go into Egypt until the evil device was over.

By His wisdom, God allowed His Son to be killed at the appointed time. God had already spoken through Prophet Isaiah and many other prophets concerning His Son:

"I shall see of the travail of His soul and shall be satisfied, by his knowledge shall my righteous servant justify many: for he shall bear their iniquities," Isaiah 53:11.

Satan never knew the wisdom of God behind the death that was to fall upon Christ. He entered into the heart of the Jewish people and rose up hostilities that culminated in the killing of Christ on the cross. There was jubiliation in the kingdom of darkness. But alas! Christ arose from the dead. He emerged victorious over death and the grave. The grave could not hold Him bound.

The scripture throws light on the essence of Christ's death and resurrection:

"But he was wounded for our transgressions, he was bruised for our iniquities: The chastisement of our peace was upon him; and with his stripes we are healed", Isaiah 53:5. It is for our justification, for healing us from our sicknesses and sins through the stripes given to Christ and His blood shed that God permitted His Son to suffer and die for us.

By the eventual physical shedding of this precious BLOOD of Christ which was predetermined before the foundation of the world, mankind has overcome satan and all his problems (sin):

101

"And they overcame him by the blood of the Lamb and by the word of their testimony; and they loved not their lives unto the death", Revelation 12:11.

To be truly an overcomer and beneficiary of this salvation, "thou shall confess with thy mouth the Lord Jesus, and shalt believe in thy heart that God raised him from the dead, thou shalt be saved. For with the heart man believeth unto righteousness: and with the mouth confession is made unto salvation", Romans 10:9;10.

It is important to note that the promise of God against satan at the garden of Eden, Genesis 3:15, had been fulfilled by the coming and eventual death of Christ. Satan can neither stand the NAME nor the BLOOD of Christ. By this, satan has been bruised. But one must have accepted by faith the Lordship of Christ and His resurrection for ones salvation and justification.

With Christ death, God's children can now be loaded into that singular seed that can never be overcome by the evil one (satan) who deceived Adam and Eve. To be part of this seed we must accept Christ:

"But as many as received him, to them he gave power to become the sons of God, even to them that believe on his name", John 1:12.

It is because of the love God has for man whom He created in His own image that He sent Christ:

"For God so loved the world that He gave his only begotten Son, that whosoever believeth

102

in him shall not perish. For God sent not his son into the world not to condemn the world, but that the world through him might be saved", John 3:16,17.

Christ was not sent to condemn us, but rather that we may be reconciled to God. Our relatinship with God was affected at the Garden of Eden through Lucifer (Satan's) temptation. So in Christ, God is with us:

"To wit, that God was in Christ reconciling the world unto himself, not imputing our trespasses unto us, and hath committed unto us the word of reconciliation",2 Corinthians 5:19.

This plan of salvation for the human race is a great exercise of God's wisdom. Thus, the death sentence that was placed upon man as a result of Satan's temptation and Adam's sin has been removed and life eternal has been given man. But this eternal life is only for those who accept the gospel - God's widsom.

Let us pause a while and try to reason into the wisdom of our God for allowing sin and Lucifer when he sinned. Doubtless, many would have been wondering and pondering over this matter. Some have asked, why did God allow Lucifer to corrupt man, and why did He not destroy Lucifer when he sinned?

God purposely allowed sin and satan to run their course for a while. Our God is good, merciful and powerful, but He is also LOVE. Each created being was endowed with freedom of choice. **GOD WANTS PEOPLE TO SERVE HIM BECAUSE THEY CHOOSE TO DO SO AND**

The state of man

NOT BECAUSE THEY CANNOT DO OTHERWISE.

God's government is based on LOVE. If satan had been destroyed immediately he sinned, heavenly beings would have served God with fear. Every responsible moral creature of God is given time to judge the extent of satan's rebellion.

Christ's life and death exposed satan's true nature and the result of sin. At the right time, God will certainly destroy satan and sin with the consent of the universe.

God is just permitting satan to run his course. IMPORTANTLY, before satan is destroyed, everyone would have had the opportunity to choose to accept Christ and live for ever. Satan's destruction will take place before the earth is recreated after the second coming of Christ.

There will be a sinless world. The destruction of satan and sin will be final. Those who have truly chosen Christ shall live gloriously forever.

Ours is a just God. By this wisdom He is not forcing Himself upon anyone. The activities of the devil has been known. He has been so exposed. Also, the truth of salvation, Christ the wisdom of God has been known. The way of Lucifer (Satan) is eternal death, but the way of God is eternal life through Christ. The choice is yours. Those who have chosen to serve God by accepting the gospel and walking in the light of that gospel have truly become God's children (they have of their volition chosen Him as their God and He will ever be with them). And those who refuse Him and His wisdon (Christ) have on

The state of man

their own (not being forced) chosen eternal death. Both satan and those who have chosen the way of sin will be finally destroyed to give way for a sinless world. The destruction of satan and sin will be the end of God's patience for sin and sinners.

You can now see the wisdom of God for allowing satan when he sinned - that God wants every created being to serve Him because they choose to. All creatures will live in absolute obedience to God after the destruction of satan and his followers. God is just and His judgement is just. Wherever Lucifer has set his foot upon since the creation, will be purged:

"But the day of the Lord will come as a thief in the night, in which the heavens shall pass away with great noise and the element shall melt with fervent heat, the earth also and the works that are therein shall be burnt up," 2 Peter 3:10.

The entire creation shall be completely purged to give room for a new heaven and a new earth where righteousness dwells.

DIVINE AND WORDLY WISDOM

The scripture says, "Who is a wise man and endowed with knowledge among you? Let him shew out of a good conversation his works with meekness of wisdom. But if ye have bitter envying and strife in your hearts, glory not, and lie not against the truth. This wisdom descendeth not from above, but is earthly, sensual and devilish. For where envying and strife is, there is confusion and every evil work. But the wisdom

105

that is from above is first pure, then peaceable, gentle and easy to be entreated, full of mercy and good fruits, without partiality and without hypocrisy", James 3:13-17.

The wisdom being spoken of here, are of two types: The **wordly wisdom, and the divine wisdom.**

The worldly wisdom is described to be earthly. This means, it is not of heaven; it is sensual and that means it is given up to the pleasures of the senses; it is devilish, meaning, that it is wicked. This is the kind of wisdom that is exercised now and again by carnally-minded people. This wisdom when applied encourges strife, envy confusion, lust, murder and every evil work.

Worldly wisdom is the wisdom applied to cheat one another. Fraudsters for instance, are well versed in this wisdom to trick and cheat individuals, companies and government. They know best how to manipulate and falsify documents and figures. By these they so much enrich themselves. Most often, these same people come back to become highly recognised and even representative of opinions of the people and that of govenment. These are clever applications of wisdom.

Some manufacturers and traders also apply wordly wisdom. They know the tricks of the trade. The result is that some goods are either manufactured substandardly or fake. The feelings and health of consumers are not put into consideration. To them, the end justifies the

The state of man

means. Unknowing consumers are adversely affected by these sharp practices. These are applications of wisdom.

Men, women, and students apply such wisdom to cheat on each other. This explains why there are so much immorality in society -husband cheating wife and vice versa- often resulting in divorce; Licentious men with wealth and position seduce young avid girls; students cheat on themselves and also cheat parents; there is examination malpractices; people commit murder and join into secret cults for wealth, position and protection; people assasinate, kidnap and abduct others; politicians also apply these kind of wisdom by given themselves unfair advantage over their rivals, fishing for compliments, currying favour, playing to the gallery and making unctious speeches and promises. All these are summed up as worldly wisdom. They are wrongly applied wisdom. Such wisdom brings confusion, wars, starvation, hardship, hurtfulness, envy, social,political ,economic and religous upheaval. This wisdom is destructive, impure and absurd. Those who exercise it are wicked and foolish Says the scriptures:

"For the wisdom of this world is foolishness with God," 1 Corinthinas 3:19.

Those who revel in these wisdom are ignorant and rebellious against the divine wisdom which comes from the right application of the **WORD** of God.

Jesus Christ said:

"And every one that heareth these sayings

The state of man

of mine, and doeth then not, shall be likened unto a foolish man, which built his house upon the sand: And the rain decended, and the floods came and the winds blew, and beat upon that house; and it fell: and great was the ruin of it", Matthew 7:26,27. The wisdom of such a person who ignores and rebels against the word of God is destructive and fruitless.

Solomon's wisdom made him have victory round about, both within and without Israel. He had honour so much that people from far and near came to see and witness the wisdom and glory that exuded from him. A nation which is ruled by wise men is strong and prosperous. In such a nation, there is spiritual richness - love, joy, meekness, purity, peace, gentleness, mercy, impartiality, compassion beside material possession. There is also economic, political and social stability in such a nation. These are possible because the leaders and the subjects of such a nation rightly apply wisdom.

Also a family operating in this wisdom is prosperous. There is abundant peace, joy, love and progress in such a home. Therefore, the living should embrace this wisdom and retain it. They should be truly doers of the WORD of GOD.

FAITH

The living needs faith to be able to worship God. Without faith it is impossible to please Him.

Faith is putting on of Christ and a complete confidence in His blood for justification. Galatians 3:26,27, says:

The state of man

"For ye are all the children of God by faith in Christ Jesus.For as many of you that have been baptised into Christ, have put on Christ."

Romans 3:25:

"Whom God hath set forth to be a propitiation through faith in his blood to declare his righteousness for the remission of sins that are past, through the forbearance of God."

PRAISING GOD

Only the living can praise God. The dead cannot. Our God is the God of the living. King Hezekiah acknowledged that when God spared and increased his life span. He declared in Isaiah 38:18-19:

"For the grave cannot praise thee, death cannot celebrate thee, they that go down into the pit cannot hope for thy truth.

The living, he shall praise thee, as I do this day! The father to the children shall make known thy truth."

David declared in psalm 104:33:

" I will sing unto the LORD as long as I live. I will sing praises to my God while I have my being. My meditation of Him shall be sweet: I will be glad in the LORD."

Also, Paul advises us, to, "rejoice in the Lord always and again I said rejoice," Philipians 4:4.

There is power in praise. Praising God and rejoicing always in Him brings heaven into hell. A praiseless life and a life full of worries and unhappiness is like hell. Many people endlessly worry about one thing or another. Our Lord Jesus Christ declared:

"Let not your heart be troubled,ye believe in God believe also in me," John 14:1. This is a very encouraging and spiritually uplifting assurance. But many people fail to realise that Jesus can set them free from the heart-aches others and troubles of life give them.

Problems can come, but through praises and gladness we can be ushered into peace. Because of Jesus, even death is swallowed up in victory. This is the truth. It is not His will for us to live in continued grief and sorrow when we come into diffcult places. God wants us to believe He is working in our lives for good. He wants us to trust Him.

Our hearts can quickly become troubled if we open our minds to lustful thoughts. That one trouble then acts as a magnet to pick others. God knows our frame:

"For we are His workmanship created in Christ Jesus unto good works which God hath before ordained that we should walk in them", Ephesians 2:10. Jesus knows that our bodies and minds are not designed by God to carry troubles. If we persist on carrying them, we suffer many things. Jesus Declared:

"If the son therefore shall make free, ye shall be free indeed", John 8:36.

We must be willing to accept His will. After all, His yoke is easy and His burden light. It is satan's yoke that is tough to bear. Therefore, the living in the Lord should live in constant praise

110

and joy of the **LORD.**

ACCEPTING GOD'S GRACE

Ours is a God of Grace. Grace is the kindness by which God bestows favours and blessings upon the ill-deserving, grants to sinners pardon of their offences. Grace is the last word He offered. Man did not deserve this grace, but he needs it, and only God can give it.

Grace is an expression of God's love and everlasting compassion for sinners:

"For God so loved the world, that he gave his only begotten son, that whosoever believeth in him should not perish, but have everlasting life", John 3:16.

The Grace of God that brings about Salvation has always been available. A time came when the wickedness of man was so much in the earth that God decided to punish by destroying the entire race with water. There was no need for everyone to die. God's grace was available to those who accepted it. The Bible says, that:

"Noah found grace in the eyes of the LORD," Genesis 6:8. The acceptance of God's grace involves action on the part of Noah:

"By faith Noah, being warned of God of things not seen as yet, moved **with fear**, prepared an ark to the saving of his house, by the which he condemned the world, and became heir of the righteousness which is by faith",Hebrew 11:7.

What readily comes to mind is the story of the prodigal son told in luke 15:11-32. It is a story of a father and two sons. One of the sons was

111

stubborn and grasping. He was caught up in the life of pleasure. Having thought deeply, planned and prepared to leave home, he asked for and received his own part of his father's inheritance and it was given to him.

Initially, everything went well. Least did he know that a fool and his money are soon parted. Soon he squandered all he had in reckless living. His friends deserted him and he was alone in the world of uncertainty and terrible lack. But he must make a living, The only job he could find was on a farm feeding hogs. He could not make enough even to eat and he was terribly whelmed by hunger ; Even "he would fain have filled his belly with husks that the swines did eat; and no man gave unto him," Luke 15:16.

One day, the reality of his situation dawned on him. A heaven-inspired thought came to his mind. He looked at himself, looked at his surroundings, reflected at his life. He was startled. "He said to himself, how many hired servants of my father's have breed enough and to spare, and I perish with hunger," Luke 15:17. With tears rolling down from his eyes, he had come to conclusion.

This man at once put his new light into action:

"I will arise and go to my father, and I will say unto him, Father, I have sinned against heaven, and before thee, and I am no more worthy to be called thy son; make me as one of thy hired servants ," Luke 15:18,19. He had made a decision and he headed home. In the distance,

The state of man

he could see his Father's home. Thoughts started creeping into his mind: Was his Father still alive? What about his dear old mother? Just then someone stepped out of the house and on recognising him, ran towards him . It was his father. He threw his arm around his son. Both were shedding tears on each other. The son tries to give his speech. With tear-drops and guilty ridden penitent voice, he said:

"Father, I have sinned against heaven, and in thy sight, and am no more worthy to be called thy son, make me as one of thy hired servants".

6But before he could go on, his father burst out with a spontaneous speech:

"Bring forth the BEST ROBE, and put on him and put a ring on his hand, and shoes on his feet: and bring hitherto, the fatted calf, and kill it; let us eat and make merry: for this my son was dead, and is alive again; he was lost, and is found. And they began to be merry", Luke 15:22-24.

Certainly, you must be touched by this story, This is the example to follow. The living truly needs to make a total return to God:

"For all have sinned and come short of the glory of God," Romans 3:23.

Accept God's grace. He will lead you in the steps to God and heaven:

"Righteousness shall go before him; and shall set us in the way of his footsteps", Psalm 85:13.

The state of man